MARRIAGE
DEAD OR ALIVE

Adolf Guggenbühl-Craig

MARRIAGE

DEAD OR ALIVE

Translated by Murray Stein

Spring Publications, Inc.
Dallas, Texas

ACKNOWLEDGMENTS

I wish to thank Murray Stein for translating this book from the Swiss edition, *Die Ehe ist tot—Es lebe die Ehe*, and also to thank Caroline Weening for editing help and composing, Robert Weening for assistance, and Robert Hinshaw for supervision of the English edition.

A.G.-C.
June 1977

Published by Spring Publications, Inc.;
P.O. Box 222069; Dallas, Texas 75222
Printed in the United States of America

Cover design by Maribeth Lipscomb and Patricia Mora

International Distributors:
Spring; Postfach; 8800 Thalwil; Switzerland.
Japan Spring Sha, Inc.; 1-2-4, Nishisakaidani-Cho;
Ohharano, Nishikyo-Ku; Kyoto, 610-11, Japan.
Element Books Ltd; Longmead Shaftesbury;
Dorset SP7 8PL; England.

Library of Congress Cataloging-in-Publication Data

Guggenbühl-Craig, Adolf.
  Marriage—dead or alive.

  Translation of: Die Ehe ist tot—lang lebe die Ehe.
  1. Marriage. 2. Individuality. I. Title.
HQ739.G78313 1986   306.8'1   86-10054
ISBN 0-88214-309-3

CONTENTS

TO

ANNE

WAR AND PEACE IN MARRIAGE

Once when Zeus and Hermes clothed themselves in mortal form and journeyed through the country of Bithynia, every door stayed closed to them and no home offered them hospitality. On the slope of a hillock overlooking a particularly inhospitable city they found the modest hut of a poor, elderly couple named Baucis and Philemon. Here the door was opened, and the old couple took them in with great friendliness. During the meal the hosts noticed that the wine was not diminishing in the least bit, but rather in a wondrous fashion kept replenishing itself in the pitcher. It soon dawned on them that their guests could not be mere mortals, whereupon the two Gods revealed their true identities. They led the elderly pair to the highest point of the hill; from there they looked about and discovered that down in the deep valley the inhospitable town had disappeared into a lake. At the same time their hut had turned into a temple, and Zeus promised them any favor they might ask. Baucis and Philemon wished only that they be allowed to spend the rest of their lives serving in the temple and that in the end one of them would not have to live longer than the other. Zeus granted them this wish, and Baucis and Philemon busied themselves about the temple for the rest of their lives. When they died, one was transformed into an oak, the other into a linden tree, and these grew up side by side.

The so-called "Holy Family" is known to us from the New Testament. Composed of Mary, Joseph, and the Christ child, it is described in numerous legends and depicted in countless pictures. In this family, peace and understanding invariably reign. Sometimes one sees Jesus in the manger, at other times in Mary's

1

lap, or playing, while she happily looks after him and Joseph stands beside them. Even external persecution, which forces them to flee temporarily to Egypt, is unable to disturb the peaceful harmony of the Holy Family. All images of this family express piety, harmony, and reciprocal love.

The secularized holy family greets us with happy smiles in popular marriage books or in advertisements for marriage trousseaus; it even serves to enliven television advertisements. We see the happy young couple strolling through a flowery meadow, while the playful, high-spirited child romps about with a small puppy. Everyone in the family is happy and satisfied. Of course, their good spirits derive from causes that are this-worldly in character. They are satisfied because they understand one another particularly well, or because their clothes are laundered with a particular detergent, or because they eat Granola every morning. For this happy family there is nothing but light, congeniality, joy, and smiles full of mutual love for one another.

Thus Baucis and Philemon, the Holy Family, the happy family of the marriage books, the beaming, satisfied couple of the TV ads each in its own way represents the "happy marriage". We speak not infrequently of "happy marrieds" and can often read in obituary notices that someone "enjoyed a happy marriage". One wishes newlyweds a "happy marriage".

The work of many psychologists and marriage counselors is determined by a somewhat more differentiated image of the happy marriage. Neurotic processes can be cleared up and "blocked communications channels can be scrubbed clean". Marriage problems must be solved. The marriage partners are to come together in a clarified, mature relationship. The neurotic marriage becomes a healthy one. A happy marriage is the goal of the efforts expended by the psychological specialist.

Since time immemorial, however, there have been other images of married life. For the Greeks, Hera and Zeus represent *the* married couple. As the Queen of Heaven, Hera is the Goddess of marriage and childbearing.

The story of this divine marriage is anything but peaceful. The parents were against the marriage, yet for all that Zeus insinuated himself into the chamber of Hera in the form of a cuckoo, in order to seduce her. In the end Hera bore him three children, one of whom was the lethal God of war, Ares. One time, for some unknown reason, Hera bound Zeus up with the help of Athena and Poseidon, and helpers had to be summoned from Tartarus to free him. Zeus himself, on the other hand, hung Hera by the wrists from the rafters of heaven and tied an anvil to her feet so that the hang-up would be sufficiently painful.

Prior to his marriage, Zeus had countless love adventures, which, without any compunction on his part, he pursued further during his marriage. Neither humans nor nymphs nor Goddesses were safe from his advances. Hera avenged herself in the most grisly fashion against these lovers of her husband, even though she herself was not immune to every attack upon her chastity. The fierce nature of this Goddess of marriage is shown in the following stories.

Before his marriage Zeus was friends with Leto, the mother of Artemis and Apollo. Hera hated Leto, even though this liaison with Zeus occurred before his marriage to Hera, and the Goddess swore that Leto would find no peace. It was only with the greatest effort that Poseidon was able to somewhat relieve Leto's suffering.

Zeus was already married to Hera when he seduced Io, the daughter of Inachus. For revenge, Hera thereupon transformed Io into a cow. Still not satisfied, she turned on the cow a gadfly, a gigantic insect which drove Io to madness. In complete panic the unfortunate Io, as a cow, raced through large parts of the world.

When Zeus took up a relationship with Kadmus' daughter Semele, Hera talked this girl into asking Zeus to show himself to her in his full magnificence, which meant certain death for the unwitting Semele.

Once Zeus slept with the beloved Aegina, for which Hera slew nearly all of the inhabitants of the island named after her.

It was also irritating to Hera when Zeus became independently creative and without the help of his mate, or of any other woman either, brought forth a daughter, Athena. For revenge Hera bore the monster Typhon, who grew up to be a dangerous enemy to her husband.

Zeus was unfaithful to Hera not only with women but also with young boys. Ganymede and Phaon were supposed to have been lovers of his.

The marriage of Zeus and Hera can hardly be reframed into a "happy one". And yet Hera is the Goddess of marriage. Hera and Zeus could be described as quarrelsome predecessors of the Holy Family. For the Greeks they symbolized marriage *par excellence.*

The image of the strife-filled marriage is mirrored, however, not only among the Gods, but also in popular stories about mortals. The strained relations between Socrates and his wife Xanthippe, for example, are legendary. Many stories are told of the quarrelsome and demanding Xanthippe, but Socrates himself, despite his wisdom, must have been a most disagreeable husband. Just how heartlessly he conducted himself vis-à-vis his wife is told in the story of his death: surrounded by his friends, Socrates prepared himself for death and reached for the goblet of hemlock; when his wife began weeping brokenheartedly, Socrates asked his friends to take away the "weepy creature".

Images and jokes, both ancient and modern, on the subject of marriage present it frequently in this unhappy form. Thus men today speak among one another of the "old lady," or the "dragon," etc. In numerous cartoons we see the wife standing behind a door, arm upraised with a rolling-pin in her hand, waiting as her husband winds his way home in a slightly drunken stupor from the local pub. In popular ballads throughout Christendom is found the theme of the ill-natured wife, whom even the devil will not take after her death.

The brutal husband who beats his wife plays hardly any part at all today in the popular imagination. In contrast, the image of the boring husband who morning and evening hides behind the newspaper is ubiquitous. And many jokes make fun of the husband who has all he can do to keep his eyes from wandering toward young girls. Then of course the cuckolded husband is a favorite butt of jokes.

It seems remarkable to me, however, that in these particularly negative and widely disseminated images of marriage, one rarely is led to question marriage itself. But this is no longer true in many modern films and literary productions. Bergman's recent film, "Scenes From A Marriage", presents the idea that a genuinely human relationship is scarcely possible within a marriage. The two main characters in this film learn to understand each other really only after they have separated.

For many modern social critics, marriage itself is a hypocritical, restrictive, destructive institution. It can be kept up only by falsehood and deceit. Often it is seen also as an instrument of the dominant social order to condition people toward servility and a slave mentality.

We must ask ourselves, therefore: is marriage a dying institution? May it even be an instrument of torture on the part of society?

MARRIAGE AND FAMILY: SOCIETY'S INSTRUMENT OF TORTURE OR A DYING INSTITUTION?

It requires no particularly original or keen spirit to discern that family and marriage are today caught up in a state of dissolution, even though many people still get married with great enthusiasm. But in all countries where laws do not make it too difficult to obtain a divorce, many marriages are being dissolved. Granted, there is as yet no country where more than half of the marriages end in divorce. Of course it is not *only* legal restraint that keeps married couples from divorce; many marriages and families are held together by purely materialistic considerations. For almost all social classes—excepting the very rich and the very poor—a divorce usually means a decline in the standard of living for both partners and for the children. The same income, after the divorce, must support two households. In social groups where money is no concern, where a divorce brings no significant decline in standard of living, over half of the marriages end in divorce.

Even when a marriage has become miserable, many couples do not divorce because of the children. "We are waiting until the children grow up," it is called. And when the children have grown up they still do not get divorced, not because the marriage relationship has improved, but because the marriage partners are too tired and are afraid of loneliness, or they believe they will no longer be able to find new partners.

Despite the rising divorce rate, most people experience divorce as a failure. At the time of the marriage one did have the intention of staying together until death would do the parting. If the courts do the separating, it means that things did not come out the way one envisioned.

It would be tiresome to give statistics on frequency of divorce in various countries, cultures, and social strata. It is much more impressive for the individual to let pass through his mind acquaintances, relatives, and friends who are somewhat over forty-five years old. In doing this one realizes with sadness — or with secret satisfaction if one is himself divorced — that many marriages which began auspiciously are no longer in existence. Often the marriages ended, childless, after several years; often there were already children present. Everyone also knows married couples who dissolve their family after fifteen, twenty, or twenty-five years of marriage. It can involve childless couples or six-children families. And just when one has calmly concluded that at least that old schoolfriend Jack and his wife Louise are enjoying a happy marriage, the telephone rings and Jack shares his decision to get a divorce.

All these divorces would not be so bad if one could at least discern unalloyed happiness and joy among the undivorced. But this is not the case. One knows from general studies as well as from personal experience that many married people manage to hold the family together only with great difficulty, by denying themselves everything that is dear to them. Here and there, nevertheless, one does meet married people who are genuinely satisfied with each other. At least they themselves think that this is the case. The objective observer often has another opinion: the marriage seems to function so well only because at least one of the partners sacrifices himself completely and neglects his own development. Either the wife sacrifices all of her personal and cultural claims for the sake of her husband's profession and comfort; or—and this is becoming ever more frequently the case—the husband serves his wife and hardly dares express his own opinions in her presence. He sacrifices his friends and his professional opportunities and practically allows his power-addicted wife to use him as a servant. How often one observes how interesting, witty, and animated the married person is when alone, but then, with the marriage partner present, every sign of liveliness vanishes. Many marriage partners who have a good marriage from an external point of view in fact virtually cripple one another.

Despite armies of psychologists and marriage counselors, not only do divorces continue to occur with great frequency, but even the marriages that still exist often seem to be nothing but growth-stunting situations. Psychiatrists and psychologists have drawn their conclusions from this unpleasant situation: marriage and family dynamics are explained to the patients. It is often doubted whether marriage and family in their contemporary form are still meaningful institutions. Is not marriage, as social revolutionaries explain it, mostly just an instrument of society used to stupefy the people?

Even psychiatrists and psychologists who do not share this radical viewpoint add debits daily to the case against marriage and family. In the cases of most neurotic patients, the cause of emotional suffering is traced back to the sick marriage compromises of their parents, to a suppressed mother or to a hen-pecked father, to every kind of unhappy family constellation.

A psychoanalysis has two goals: to free the patient from his neurotic suffering, and further, to help him toward his own full development and toward finding the meaning of his life. Very often, however, psychoanalysis ends a marriage with a divorce. To find meaning in life means, in this case, first of all determining that the marriage does not allow any sort of meaningful development for the analysand.

Many modern writers describe marriage as a sick institution held together only by lies and hypocrisy, mutual deception and self-deception. Family life, then, would consist in an endless two-way torment. The mendacity and hypocrisy in the so-called bourgeois marriage is one of the favorite targets of modern authors. In this view one might be tempted to paraphrase Shakespeare's Hamlet: Something is rotten indeed—not in Denmark, but in family and marriage.

If one looks at the institution of marriage and family with complete impartiality and fairness, the following picture emerges: if, using great psychological acuity, one were to dream up a social institution which would be unable to function in every single case and which was meant to torment its members, one would certainly invent the contemporary marriage and the institution of today's family. Two people of different sex, usually with extremely different images, fantasies, and myths, with differing strength and vitality, promise one another to be with each other night and day, so to speak, for a whole lifetime. Neither of them is supposed to spoil the other's experience, neither is supposed to control the other, both of them should develop all their potentials fully. This mighty oath is often declared, however, only because of an overwhelming sexual intoxication. Such an intoxication is wonderful, but is it a solid groundwork for a lifetime together?

It is well-known that most people get on each other's nerves even when they undertake only a fourteen-day trip together. After a few days one may hardly even express himself anymore, and every little decision turns into a querulous wrestling match. The two marriage partners, however, promise to live their whole lives (thirty, forty, fifty, sixty years) together in the greatest physical, spiritual, and psychological intimacy. And this life-long commitment they make to each other in their youth! Perhaps in ten years they are both completely different people. They make this promise at an age when they neither know who they are themselves nor who the other is. Above all, no one knows how one or the other is later going to develop. The charming, adaptable young girl turns into— who would guess it? —a power-intoxicated matron. The romantic young man with such lofty plans for the future behaves later perhaps like an irresponsible weakling.

That a decent, responsible society not only allows, but actually encourages, young people in their complete ignorance to bind themselves permanently to the psychological problems which their vows entail, seems incomprehensible.

The more life-expectancy increases, the more grotesque this situation becomes. Two hundred years ago people did not grow so very old, and most marriages ended after ten or twenty years with the death of one of the marriage partners. Today many unbroken marriages last fifty, or even sixty, years.

THE MANY FACES OF MARRIAGE AND FAMILY LIFE

It is the contemporary *Zeitgeist* that is slowly undermining marriage as an institution. The contemporary deterioration of morals, the reinterpretation or even dissolution of values, does not call halt before marriage and family. Western society finds itself in a spiritual crisis. This crisis is shaking the foundations of our social life and the foundations of marriage and family.

Such and similar conclusions are heard from circles that also have the impression that today's youth is particularly troublesome, that criminality is increasing in frightening proportions, that art is degenerating, etc. This opinion comes from those who hold that things were better in earlier times. These people are often influenced by an image of an earlier "golden age". This veneration for the past serves our understanding of most social phenomena just as little as does the longing for a new future. The people who suffer from such a longing believe that everything new is better than what was before. The one type believes that there was once a golden age; the other believes naively in progress and hopes for a future paradise.

In different historical periods, marriage and family have different meanings. All social institutions, including marriage and family, are caught up in continuous change. A marriage in the time of Zwingli's reformation in Zürich was certainly not the same as a marriage in the time of Rudolf Brun in the thirteenth century. The marriage of a rich merchant in the time of Louis XIV must be differently understood from the marriage of a well-to-do merchant in today's Paris.

In Christian lands until the Reformation, and in Catholic cultures and to some extent in Protestant cultures until recent times, there were significantly fewer divorces than today. But this does not mean that marriages were either better or worse. The bond unto death, which we even today encourage as an ideal for a married couple, was until recently taken more seriously by the courts. The integrity of a monogamous marriage in the Christian West was often only a legal fiction. Among the nobility of Western Europe in the sixteenth, seventeenth, and eighteenth centuries, for example, it was common that the husband took a mistress and the wife a lover. And in countries where until very recently divorce was impossible—as in Italy—many married couples lived separately and maintained a common household with a friend.

Scholars are not agreed on how marriage originated. Several anthropologists are fond of the fantasy that humans at first lived in herds and enjoyed complete promiscuity: every man had sexual contact with every woman; it was unknown that sexual intercourse led to pregnancy; the role of the man in the production of children was not understood; children were raised by the herd as a whole. The family, marriage, monogamous or polygamous associations, are all understood as secondary developments.

Other scholars prefer other fantasies. Marriage and family are for them primary and primordial. They believe this because many mammals have "marriages," be they monogamous or polygamous ones. The primary social structure of mankind is supposed to be mirrored in the image of a man with a cluster of wives and children around him.

Is one to look for the origins of marriage in the sexual drive, the drive to propagate the species, or is its origin related to the origin of ownership? Did men and women at some point begin to possess one another? We do not know.

Looking through history, we see that marriage and family have been variously founded and formed and differently understood. For the ancient Persian, for example, marriage had its *raison d'être* in producing warriors for the king. The production of children has played a decisive role among many peoples, even if it has not always to do with producing troops for the king. Thus Abraham, with approval from his wife, begat children with Hagar the maid, because Sarah was barren.

The nations of the earth have been brought much closer together in our time through technology. Nevertheless, the organization and conceptions of marriage and family maintain great diversity. Even the founding of a family takes place according to a variety of criteria. The romantic choice of a partner, marrying from motives of love and sexual attraction, is steadily gaining ground as a criterion, but there are still many large segments of mankind where this has created no stir at all. In India about eighty percent of the marriages are still arranged by the parents, and while a romantic connection is hoped for, it does not appear very frequently. Interestingly, these arranged marriages are neither better nor worse than those based on romantic love. Both kinds bring disappointments.

The purchase of wives is still practiced among many peoples; theft of wives, on the other hand, is no longer very widespread. The number of husbands and wives in some places is not the same. Strict monogamy is only one of many possiblities. The possession of many wives still occurs frequently in Asia and Africa. And according to some reports of travelers, polyandry (multiple husbands) apparently still exists. Even a mixture of polyandry and polygamy is described in certain areas.

Marriage is lived under the most diverse conceptions. Ethnologists describe nearly every imaginable form of family and married life. The young couple moves into the home of the husband's parents; in other places, they move to the home of the wife's parents. The husband has complete legal power over the wife, excepting the power over life and death; or, the wife has a better position under the law. We find matriarchies and patriarchies. Men live together and meet their wives only on certain specified days. Work is divided; work is done together. A minimum of sexual contact is determined by legal statute, or sexual contact is limited by the law, etc., etc.

Ethnologists also report the most diverse customs regarding the possibilities and impossibilities of divorce; divorce may be only a minor formality; divorce may be possible only when one of the partners is committing adultery; there may be no possibility of divorce under any circumstances; the initiative for a divorce proceeding may come only from the wife; among many peoples only death

14

may end a marriage. An extreme form of the indissoluble marriage bond occurs in the custom of widow incineration, in which the wife remains true to her husband even after his death by voluntarily throwing herself on his funeral pyre. Perhaps the most unusual form of marriage described by ethnologists is the following: A maiden is married by her parents to a young boy. Since a sexual life with this male child is naturally impossible, the young wife is allowed to take a lover and even to have children by him. When her husband reaches the age of sexual capability, she introduces him to sexuality. After several years the husband takes for a mistress the wife of a child-husband, and he maintains this relationship until her husband comes of age, when she introduces him to sexual life.

What we refer to as the institution of marriage and family, therefore, is not something that was and is the same among all peoples in all times. Misleading are statements like: "The family or married couple is the basic unit of human society;" "Father, mother, and child are the natural community," etc. Among certain animal species there exists a family structure that is everywhere found to be identical. This structure is created instinctively among these animals over and over again in exactly the same way. But among humans this is unequivocally not the case. Marriage and family structure are something "unnatural", not instinctive, an artificial product of human effort. Marriage is anti-natural, an *opus contra naturam*. This is why we find so many different forms of marriage in the course of history and among various cultures. Many images fix their mark on marriage and family.

At this point one could object and call all of this 'nonsense'. Children have to be raised somehow, and this takes place in the most natural fashion within the family, under the care of father and mother. Father, mother, and children constitute the primordial image of the family, and without marriage and family mankind would have died out long ago. The child needs, at least up to its twelfth or thirteenth year, the sheltering and protecting care of both parents, and the care of the next generation is the basis for the original and natural family unit. Moreover, the argument continues, it has been shown that only where there is a healthy family, a husband and wife working lovingly together, can spiritually and physically healthy children grow up. Every disturbance in the relationship between the husband and wife has a deleterious effect on the children. Looked at from the point of view of child-rearing, there can be no doubt that marriage, as we ideally conceive of it today, must be one of the most natural and most primordial human institutions imaginable.

This objection is less sound than it might appear to be at first glance. Granted, men and women must come together if children are to be produced. Still, after the ensuing conception and after the birth, various possibilities for raising the children remain for the persons involved. In various times and in different cultures and social strata, mankind has handled the task of raising and educating children in the most diverse ways. Whether the current style of raising children in the western world is really the only possibility, or even the best possibility, must remain open to question.

Perhaps the modern psychologist does not realize clearly enough that his conceptions about the conditions under which a child develops in a healthy way, and even about what a healthy development is, are conditioned and defined by images of the culture to which the psychologist belongs, are thus conditioned and defined through a mythology that is dominant for him.

Here I must become more specific. Until very recent times there were large social groups, culturally and politically very significant, whose methods of child-rearing bore little relation to the mythic image of the Holy Family. That the results of this type of child-rearing were any worse—while different they certainly were— than ours has yet to be proven. In the English aristocracy, for example, at least for those individuals who possessed wealth and property, it was customary until recent times to give the children over to a nanny as soon as possible after birth. This nanny, not the mother or the father, took on the care of the child. The parents removed themselves in every way possible from the job of child-rearing. The boys, and to some extent also the girls, when they had outgrown their nanny and nursemaids, were immediately sent off to boarding school, where they lived with children of the same age and were raised by a group of men or women. The father devoted himself to the management of the estate or made a career as a colonial official, a military officer, or a wastrel. The mother looked to social life for her satisfaction. Similar circumstances existed also among the French aristocracy.

We can conclude that there are various possiblities for the rearing and education of children. The kind of family-centered rearing that we imagine toady as the ideal is in no sense the only way, and in all probability it is not unambiguously better or worse than other ways. Every educational system has its advantages and disadvantages. The English aristocratic system perhaps encouraged the development of a somewhat detached, impersonal human being, who could persevere with a certain toughness through the most diverse circumstances, whether as district commissioner in Africa or as colonial official in India. The painstaking parental control which we exert over our young from their infancy through their adolescence forms persons who have strong feelings and personal attachments but who tend to be continually disillusioned by the big, bad world when once they observe that not all other people are as loving as "mom" and "dad". The drawback of our system of rearing is perhaps narcissistic pampering; the advantage, on the other hand, is an increased capacity for personal love.

The "best system" for child-rearing does not exist. The Roman upper classes, who wanted to make their children into fit soldiers and capable statesmen, had to raise their children differently from the early Christians, for whom the major concern was to make it possible for their children to learn of God and to attain paradise. Children of totalitarian states, such as the Soviet Union, must be raised differently from children of a democratic state, such as Denmark, for example.

The goals of our educational and rearing efforts change practically every ten to twenty years into something completely different. Since the goals are continuously changing, it is almost impossible to examine the efficacy of a particular education. Today it is such that no sooner has a particular style of education been worked out than the goal of education has changed, because a new image of man has come along. Since "other people" are always being wished for, one is unable to make a judgment about the results of education.

Pedagogy is not an objective science. Even those educators who give the appearance of being scientific are children of their times, and create educational systems that conform to the expectations of a time-bound image of man.

Since we never have enough time to test the results of our efforts, the various systems of education express simply our own fantasies and conceptions about education, answering to the question of how children are to be formed into the adults we wish them to be.

Looked at from the viewpoint of caring for children, it is questionable whether our current image of the family is a "natural" or necessary one. I believe that we will get closer to an understanding of marriage and family once it becomes clear to us that marriage and family are artificial creations, expressions of human fantasy, human works in the truest sense of the word and far removed from any sort of "natural" instinct.

When we speak in this book of marriage, we understand that marriage, as it is currently experienced in Western Europe and the United States, is a social institution that is continuously changing. It is the result of a long historicial development and of constantly changing philosophical, religious, political, social, and economic conceptions and attitudes.

The contemporary marriage is still understood as a life-long commitment. Divorce is possible but not wished for. The dominant conception today is that in marriage two more or less equally qualified partners bind themselves together for life. The position of the wife is legally distinguished from that of the husband, at least in Switzerland, in that the husband is responsible for support and maintenance. This burden is evened out by certain rights: the husband gives the family his name; his place of residence becomes that of the wife; he has the final word on educating the children, and he usually controls the money. In the opinion of many citi-

19

zens, the laws concerning marriage are somewhat antiquated. There are efforts under way to establish clearly and firmly the full equality of husband and wife in the eyes of the law. That the marriage laws are somewhat *passé* should in no way be a rebuke to the creators of the Swiss code of civil law. Most of the laws that have to do with social institutions must necessarily become somewhat antiquated. The conceptions and images on which social institutions rest change pretty rapidly. Laws should not be altered too quickly to reflect these social changes, otherwise the continuous changing of the laws would create uncertainty as to what one's legal rights are.

Moreover, according to current conceptions, husband and wife—and children also—should be able to develop their full psychological potential. That both should develop themselves in this way is neither self-evident nor natural; it is one of the time-bound conceptions that may change one day. Today we view equality between marriage partners as self-evident, but we cannot know if even in a hundred years the greater part of mankind will find it correct for wife or husband to be treated as a partner with inferior rights.

WELL-BEING AND SALVATION

The distinction between well-being and salvation is artificial. In the midst of actual human life, the two cannot always be sharply distinguished. In trying to understand man, however, it is important to establish this distinction at least theoretically.

Well-Being and Salvation

Well-being has to do with the avoidance of unpleasant tensions, with striving for the possession of a physical sense of comfort, relaxed and pleasant. The state of well-being requires having sufficient nourishment, protection from the elements, an absence of anxiety about one's continuing existence, an easing of sexual tension now and then, and a pleasant though not exhausting amount of physical activity. Furthermore, it requires the possibility of satisfying some of the so-called material wishes without inordinate effort. Also a minimum of space for living is necessary.

One should not, however, understand well-being as purely physiological. A feeling of belonging to a group and enjoying a certain measure of prestige within one's collective group are necessary. Human security, a pleasant feeling of belonging to the herd, a good relationship within the family and among neighbors and relatives are indispensable. For many adults, moreover, a sense of well-being depends on the presence of one or more children.

Clearly not belonging to the state of well-being are tensions, dissatisfactions, painful emotions, anxiety, hatred, difficult and insoluble internal and external conflicts, obsessive searching for an undiscoverable truth, confused struggles about God, and the felt need to come to terms with evil and death. Sickness most certainly does not belong to the state of well-being. It is much easier, at any rate, for physically and psychologically healthy people to enjoy a sense of well-being than it is for the sick. "Give us our daily bread" really implies, "Give us daily our sense of well-being."

A correlate of well-being is happiness: a person who possesses a sense of well-being is happy and satisfied.

The government of a nation is concerned with the well-being of its citizens. For this reason we often speak of the "welfare

21

state".

The concept of salvation is familiar to us from its religious context. The Christian religion, for example, sought to bring salvation to mankind. This has to do not simply with a happy, relaxed earthly existence. In the context of religious language, salvation means seeking and finding contact with God. In philosophy one speaks of the search for meaning, for an experience of the meaning of life. In the Christian conception, salvation is not completely obtainable in this life. Sin and death burden us continually, as does the eclipse of God or our backslidings from him. Salvation involves the question of life's meaning, and this question can never be ultimately answered.

Just as there are innumerable philosophies and religions, so there are innumerable ways to salvation. In the last analysis, every individual person must seek and find salvation in his own way. All paths to salvation have, nevertheless, certain features in common. I know of none in which a confrontation with suffering and death is not necessary.

For Christians, the great mythologem for the path to salvation is the life of Jesus Christ. His works, his suffering and death belong unalterably to the path by which he found his way back to the Father. Even after his death he could not immediately ascend to heaven but had first to spend three days in the underworld.

For Buddhists Nirvana means salvation, but before a person can begin to strive for Nirvana he must be shaken by the specters of illness, old age, and death.

We can hardly ever say precisely, or even imagine, just what salvation is. We know only the various soteriological pathways. The state of salvation as such can perhaps only be intuited in a human life during the brief moments of religious or philosophical peak experiences. For just a few seconds, while watching a sunset, or standing in the shower, or in church at a baptism, or at an annual festival, one believes suddenly that he knows the meaning of life; one makes contact with his own spark of divinity.

As goals, salvation and well-being contradict each other. The path to happiness does not necessarily include suffering. For the sake of our well-being we are urged to be happy and not to break our heads with questions that have no answer. A happy person sits at his family table among his loved ones and enjoys a hearty meal. A person who seeks salvation wrestles with God, the devil, and the world, and he confronts death, even if all of this is not absolutely necessary at that precise moment.

The civil state is obliged to concern itself with the well-being of its citizens, but it is not in a position to offer anyone salvation. It can only provide each citizen with the freedom to seek salvation as the spirit moves him to do so. It is the churches and religious communities that occupy themselves with salvation.

In Jungian psychology and psychotherapy a fairly sharp distinction is drawn between well-being and salvation. To promote well-being involves helping the patient to adapt to his environment and to learn to make his way successfully through the world. It also has to do with freeing him so far as possible from neurotic patterns. But we speak further of "individuation" in Jungian psychology. This does not necessarily concern mental health, well-being, or a sense of happiness. Individuation involves the striving of a person to find his own pathway of salvation. As a healer, the psychotherapist seeks to help the patient toward a feeling of well-being and happiness in this world. He seeks also to support the patient in his search for salvation, for individuation. The path of individuation, therefore, has a lot to do with salvation and little to do with well-being.

For the exposition which follows it is essential to understand exactly what we mean by the image or concept of individuation, this psychological description of the pathway of salvation. In order to avoid misunderstanding I must furnish some more background. Since the beginning of man's existence he has been trying to find out who he is and what motivates him. Psychology as a science is still very young, but most likely man has always wondered about the soul. This sort of wondering is related to what we describe as religion. Psychology and religion can be seen as beginning with the realization of death: this was accompanied by images and fantasies, from which evolved rituals of burial. The conscious knowledge of death was responsible for the creation of religion and psychology.

In our western world we know this "religious psychology," this searching and researching the nature of the soul within a religious framework, most clearly in its Christian form and to some extent also in its Greek and Roman mythological forms. Jesus Christ was certain that God was about to enter history and lead mankind home to His kingdom. The soul had to be understood from this eschatological standpoint. The saving of souls was, therefore, the primary concern of medieval Christianity. The point of knowing about the soul was to enable a person to advance his soul heavenward and to prevent it from falling into eternal damnation.

During the Renaissance and afterwards, the dominance of the Christian God began to give way. A new myth named science raised its head. Man now sought to observe objectively what he had once described as God's creation, in order to discover "just how things are in themselves" without any further aims. This so-called objective method of observation influenced the investigators of the soul. The soul, which once one wanted to know about in order to save, was now placed, so to speak, under the microscope. Objective experimental observation became in time *the* psychological method. Unfortunately, everything that was even vaguely associated with the old religious psychology or with the soul's salvation was discarded in this counter-reaction. No indefinite religious objectives of the soul's existence were to disturb the clarity of observation. The single motivating power that was attributed to psychological life was the survival instinct of the individual and of the species. An effort was made to understand psychological life as a bundle of more or less successful survival mechanisms. Psychological research took place within a biological model.

Freud, the "Christopher Columbus of psychology", believed in this biological model. He described a soul that could be pressed into the old biological model only by a fanatical faith in science. And Freud remained a true believer! Hunger, thirst, aggression, and sexuality had to remain the ruling Gods. Yet Freud often felt uncomfortable in his biological dogmatism. He observed powers at work in the world of the soul that would not allow themselves to be pressed into the survival mode. Thus Freud polarized, finally, the basic human instincts. All drives that seemed to support life he named Eros, and beside these he postulated the opposite drive, the so-called death-drive, Thanatos.

C.G. Jung, who was first friendly, then hostile toward Freud, freed psychology from the narrowness of classical biological thinking. Yet he worked to some extent with the methods of natural science: he observed the life of the psyche in himself and in others

25

with great care and objectivity. He wanted to remain an objective scientist. In a still broader sense Jung was objective: he freed himself from the timidity of his predecessors who, out of fear of falling into some sort of religious fog, wanted by dogmatic means to reduce all of psychological life to the biological instincts of preservation. Jung was free of the compulsion to subsume on dogmatic grounds every psychological phenomenon under the rubric of biology. Using the method of unprejudiced observation, he discovered the following: the creations, the joys and sorrows, the images and desires of the psyche could not be reduced to the so-called basic instincts of hunger, thirst, aggression, and sexuality. Another power, another drive, had to be brought into consideration. Jung named this power the drive to individuation.

Since Jung, other notable psychologists have recognized the individuation drive. Concepts were invented such as "the search for meaning," "the search for individual identity," "self-realization," "creativity," "the other dimension," etc., all of which are still somewhat vague and undefined.

INDIVIDUATION: NOT ELITIST, ALWAYS POLITICAL

What makes the Jungian concept of individuation useful for the psychological life of persons is, above all, the *detailed* description of it.

Individuation is a process, but it can also be understood as a drive. Individuation is as essential a part of human motivation as hunger, thirst, aggression, sexuality, and pressures toward finding relaxation and attaining happiness. Jung underscored certain aspects of individuation over and over again. He stressed the importance of the development of the individual soul which, to be sure, has its roots in the collective soul, but which nevertheless must differentiate itself from this and develop itself individually. He often wrote of the importance of becoming conscious; over and over again he insisted that conscious and unconscious aspects of the personality should be integrated. He associated individuation very strongly with a process that we observe in analysis, yet he never assumed that individuation could be found only in the analytical context.

The drive to individuation impels us to make contact with an inner spark of divinity, which Jung described as the self.

The process and goal of individuation can only be indicated by symbols. The life of Jesus Christ, for example, insofar as it can be understood symbolically, can be conceived of as an individuation process. In religious language one could say that the goal of individuation is to approach God (or the Gods), to make contact with the world, which is at the same time one's own being.

Another symbol of individuation is the image of the "journey to the golden city, Jerusalem". In Bunyan's *Pilgrim's Progress,* this painful and courageous pilgrimage is depicted in great detail. In empirical life, we are always at the beginning or in the middle of a journey to Golden Jerusalem, never at the goal.

Fairy tales often contain individuation symbolism. The hero must undertake many adventures in order to marry the princess. This marriage is a symbol for bonding with one's own soul. A man projects the image of his soul on the feminine. In this sense, marriage in fairy tales symbolizes the goal of psychological development.

Often a "Pilgrim's Progress" turns into a "Prince's Progress"; that is, the prince allows himself to be distracted on the journey so often that the princess is dead by the time he reaches the castle.

Individuation as presented in fairy tales, unfortunately, is often too simple and undifferentiated. Ancient myths give us a better picture. I would mention here as an example the old Welsh legend of Culhrwch and Olwen. The name Culhrwch most likely means "pigs' trench". Culhrwch was born among pigs. After his birth his mother goes insane and dies. A good stepmother rears him, and from her he hears of a maiden named Olwen, the daughter of a giant. The giant will give him his daughter, however, only on the condition that he perform forty possible and impossible tasks, all of which are terrifying. Many deeds are performed by Culhrwch alone, others are accomplished with the help of his comrades, still others are done by his comrades or by King Arthur alone. In the course of these adventures, Culhrwch crisscrosses the entire known world of the Celts. The tale reaches its highpoint in the violent hunt for a wild boar and the blood-draining of a witch.

Individuation as a psychological development is often presented in pictorial art also, though too often in a form that is too neat and too tame. The image of the noble knight St. George is well-known. He is brought to our attention by painters, sculptors, and goldsmiths in churches, palaces, and private homes. High on his horse, decked out in elegant armor, the noble knight with his spear pins to the ground beneath him the writhing dragon.

Symbolically, this image shows the victorious conquest of St. George over his dark unconscious. Psychologically much more pertinent than this is how the myth of Culhrwch presents the conflict with the unconscious powers of the soul. After the victory over the mighty wild boar, the black witch is discovered in her grotto. King Arthur, as the helper of Culhrwch, sends servants into the hole; these tug at the witch by her hair. She in turn grabs them by their forelocks and throws them to the ground. Screaming, they flee from the hole. In the end Arthur has to intervene personally, and he cuts the witch in two with his sword. The blood is drained from her, most likely with the intention of drinking it and thereby gaining strength for the decisive encounter with the giant, Olwen's father. The unfortunate future father-in-law of the hero not only gets his beard shaved off but also his skin and ears; his head is knocked off and impaled. Finally the hero is able to unite himself with Olwen. Now he is joined to his soul, as it is projected onto the feminine figure.

Courage, cowardice, chaotic fighting, filth, and the gruesome imbibing of witches' blood characterize this story. In contrast, elegant detachment and distance are portrayed in the pictures of St. George and the dragon.

Individuation is better depicted and symbolized in the bloody and chaotic story of Culhrwch than in the image of the elegant knight St. George.

Individuation means an active, difficult, uncomfortable working through of one's own complex psyche towards a joining of its opposites; these opposites are symbolized by man and woman.

Individuation is a long and interesting journey. A lengthy path must be traversed until a man, for instance, has confronted and dealt with the manifold aspects of the maternal. First he has to deal with the natural, nourishing animal mother, who strikes him as conservative and anti-spiritual. Mythologically she is represented by the extraverted bearer of fertility, Demeter. What is seductive about the natural mother is that, like the gingerbread witch of Hansel and Gretel, she nourishes; what is sinister is that she would like to devour the man. Too strong a tie to the mother inhibits the development of a man.

Another side of the Goddess with which a man has to have it out is mythologically represented by Persephone, the Queen of the underworld. This is the fairy-like, *spiritual,* ambitious aspect of mother: she can inspire a man as well as drive him to death and madness. The ambitious fantasies of a man's mother can engender in him a drive toward spiritual achievements, as well as they can produce the destructiveness of overweening ambition.

It requires great psychological effort for a man to reach the point of understanding that these archetypal powers of the psyche inhere in himself, and that it avails nothing to see them only in his natural mother or to project them onto other women or onto institutions; to reach the point of seeing that nothing is accomplished by railing against his mother or by leveling repeated accusations against society. And this is only one of the prodigious lessons that must be mastered in the course of individuation.

Of even more decisive importance in the process of individuation is a man's coming to terms with a woman or with the feminine in general; and vice versa, a woman's coming to terms with a man or with the masculine. One of the greatest themes of individuation is the wondrous fact that human existence—as well as animal existence—is lived fruitfully only in the context of the masculine-feminine polarity. Love and hate, separation and union with the contrasexual figure outside and within oneself, belong to the psychological development that stands under the banner of this soteriological process.

Coming to terms with suffering and death, with the dark side of God and of his creation, with what makes us suffer, with what we use to torment ourselves and others, all of this cannot be e-vaded in the individuation process. There can be no individuation without confrontation with the destructive side of God, of the world, and of our own soul.

To be steadfast in this confrontation is very difficult both in-dividually and collectively, and every historical period finds its own methods for evading this task. In our time it is the mode to assign suffering and destruction to social causes. Simple solutions for the problems of suffering and destruction are called for: if society would be reorganized, suffering would disappear overnight. Everything that we would call "bad" is the result of poor rearing and education, and this in turn is the product of the manipulations of an evil society which is governed by a few villains for their own benefit.

Another principal form of evasion from suffering expresses itself in the belief that things are progressing. Although things are still in a bad way today, they are getting better with every passing day, and it is only a question of time—and organization—until par-adise will be established on earth.

Individuation and salvation are very closely-related concepts. The goal of individuation, one could say, is the salvation of the soul. Unfortunately, both concepts are constantly in danger of being understood much too narrowly.

Frederick the Great, the Prussian king whom I find other-wise not very sympathetic, is supposed to have said: "Everyone must become blessed in his own fashion," i.e., everyone must find salvation in his own way.

Mankind has consistently been willing to fight bloody wars for soteriological aims. Everyone believed that he had the duty to make others submit to his understanding of salvation. The darkest, most destructive shadow elements mixed themselves into the motives of the soteriological warrior. The drive to power and the frenzy of destruction hid themselves under the mantle of the motive of saving souls.

Salvation, however, is available for everyone; it is open to everyone, a possibility for every soul. Expressed in Christian language: Christ died for all men.

Salvation itself, however, can be grasped only symbolically and represented only in images. Images that express this ineffability are very different. Salvation presents itself in many ways to the eye of human understanding. While salvation is possible for and common to all souls, it can be attained by the most diverse means. The formula *Sine ecclesia nulla salus* is a tragic misunderstanding, insofar as *ecclesia* is limited to one specific community of soteriological questers.

An elitist definition tends to undermine the value of the concept or image of individuation. One supposes, for example, that individuation is open only to those who would undergo analysis. Only those who can speak about their own psychological development and understand their dreams psychologically and interpret them are capable and worthy of salvation. Such a conception begs a comparison with such Christian sects as assert that only forty thousand souls will be redeemed by Christ, with the members of that particular sect naturally included.

Individuation

Another equally presumptuous restriction lies in the claim
that only persons with a certain intelligence and a certain educational level are capable of individuating. Persons with an IQ of
less than 90, it is suggested, are not up to it.

There are innumerable paths to individuation, not only
the psychological or the intellectual. The way is open for persons to individuate through art or cooking, within the context of
love or technology, business or politics.

Just how diverse these paths of individuation can be I would
like to illustrate with the following examples.

I once listened to a black band in New Orleans, all of whose
members were at least sixty-five years old. Many could no longer
command their instruments completely since they had lost much
of the flexibility in their joints. They played an old-fashioned
kind of jazz. Listening to them and watching the different play-
ers, one had the impression that these musicians had grasped something and were saying something that had to do with individuation. They were on this soteriological pathway.

Another experience that impressed me deeply occurred when
I visited a worship service designed for mentally retarded children
by a reformed religious order. The communion was distributed to
the congregation, to the parents of the damaged children and to
the children themselves. For months before this communion service the children had been prepared and made aware of the meaning of communion through the use of pictures. What happened
within these children as they took communion we will never know
exactly. But watching their faces and trying to put oneself into
their places, one could not avoid the impression that something
happened in the souls of these disadvantaged children that came

close to individuation. Before the distribution of the communion elements, in place of a sermon, the children were shown pictures telling of the suffering, death, and resurrection of Christ. Did they understand? We could ask the same question of those of us with normal intelligence: have we grasped the suffering and resurrection of Christ? In reality, no one can grasp individuation conceptually. Only images can express it. For every participant in this worship service it was a conviction that in the moment of distribution these children intuited salvation.

On the occasion of a conference for psychologists, during which the concept of individuation was being discussed, the reaction to the question: "Can an idiot individuate? " was only a strange shaking of heads. But the question is not, *"Can* an idiot individuate? " for this is certain, but rather, *"How does* an idiot individuate? "

We have now discussed individuation and how it is represented symbolically in fairy tales, sagas, and living symbols.

Something in our presentation of individuation and of salvation could still, however, be open to misunderstanding. One aspect seems to be missing. Individuation and soteriological questing seem to be something autistic and self-centered. It seems to happen to individuals as they work on their own souls in the stillness of their private rooms: alone, or in a pair, as for instance in marriage, that intense dialectical encounter. The banal question of the philistine crops up here: what use is all of this for social institutions, for the community, for the state, in short, for one's fellow man?

Individuation is not individualism. Working together with what one abstractly and mistakenly describes today as society—

that is, working together with neighbors, local communities, organizations, toward the salvation of all one's fellow men—this all belongs to individuation.

Every single soul has a part in the collective soul. Our deepest strata are bound up with the collective unconscious, the collective soul, through which all men and groups are joined together. An egoistic individuation of a single person as a private pastime is therefore hardly conceivable.

It is noteworthy that in many fairy tales and myths having to do with individuation, the hero and his helpers or friends are kings, princes, princesses; or in archaic myths, helpful Gods, all of whom have an influence on other people.

Kings, princes, etc., are people with political functions, with high political offices. These mythical and fairy tale figures have collective and social implications. The individuation of kings must hold benefits for society. Moreover, these myths and fairy tales tell us that an individuation without social implications is unthinkable. We must fill out this social dimension of individuation above all by looking to medieval images. We want to look not only at the figures of kings and knights, but also at those of hermits and recluses. Kings and knights were active in society. The recluse, on the other hand, retreated into isolation, not only to pray for his own soul's salvation, but to struggle for the salvation of all mankind.

Participation in society always belongs together with individuation, whether in extraverted form as in the case of medieval knights, or in introverted form as in the case of the praying monk, or in mixed form. The individuating person occupies himself with his fellow man, whether by active participation or by inward struggles with the collective problems.

MARRIAGE:
ONE PATHWAY OF SALVATION

Well-being and salvation must be conceptually distinguished for the understanding of human psychology. Individuation, as C.G. Jung describes it, is that portion of human motivation that presses towards salvation.

Individuation, both the process and the soterific goal that is empirically unattainable, can only be experienced and represented through symbols. One must add that since time immemorial, mankind has sought to express its understanding of psychology through images or myths, for the reason that the behavior of humans is determined by images which momentarily gain dominance. We behave not on the basis of precise intellectual understanding or exact reflections, but rather on the basis of images that hover before us. To become conscious means to see more clearly the images that lead us, and in this endeavor we continually reflect upon and fantasy around the images that govern us.

The state of well-being is presented in various images as well. The land of the Phaeaces, as described by the Greeks, is such a picture of the state of well-being. In that land things are peaceful, and all the people seem to be happy. What is missing, however, is tension, stimulation, struggle. Odysseus is not able to hold out for long in the land of the Phaeaces!

In the stories of seafaring one frequently comes across descriptions of such lands of milk and honey. Often it is told how a seafarer lands somewhere on an island where there is always plenty to eat, where the women are at his free disposal, and where he spends all day lying about in a hammock. Such "welfare islands" are often projected into the South Seas. The stories about these seafarers are representations of inner images more than they are precise descriptions of actual experiences.

One characteristic that all these stories of happy South Sea islands and other lands of milk and honey have in common is that sooner or later the storyteller must leave that land, and even wants to leave it. Seldom on these "welfare islands" is he able really to find himself and to come to his own soul.

Related to the state of well-being is the image of so-called naturalism. One conceives of the possibility of a natural pattern of behavior, of people who are completely natural. But man is in himself *unnatural,* that is, nothing happens to him in a simple way: he always has to have fantasies, to reflect, to consider, to come to terms with his inner reactions, to question his existence. Only before the Fall was man "natural". Paradise as we imagine it, as it was before Adam and Eve bit into the forbidden fruit, is a place of "natural well-being".

The images that stand behind modern mass tourism, for instance, are closely bound to well-being and so-called naturalism. Tourist advertising leads us down the rose-strewn path of believing that tourist organizations can take us to a place where we can get rid of all tensions, desires, and struggles. The tourist organization will take care of all the unpleasant details. Good eating and drinking will be provided. Sun, warmth, and a splendid beach is reserved just for us. In the ads for such group tours it is also suggested that the tourists will get their due sexually and will need experience no frustrations in this respect.

The search for salvation and the search for well-being are not, however, altogether unrelated. It is possible that the people who are taken in by the large tourist organizations and who undertake such a journey to a welfare paradise are looking not only for the land of the Phaeaces or the land of milk and honey, but for a land where they will find their souls—searching for the land of the Greeks with their souls. The admixture of soteriological questing in modern tourism, however, is very minimal; perhaps this is the reason why the places that attract large numbers of tourists often end up with a cultural catastrophe for the local inhabitants. The indigenous peoples of the great tourist spots seem to lose their souls: all cultural, religious, and political efforts and ideals are crippled, since the culture is engaged only in luring ever more tourists. It is not the contact with an essentially foreign population that corrupts the inhabitants of the great foreign resorts; it is the contact with great masses of people who are seeking for the moment only well-being and not salvation that weakens and devalues the indigenous population.

For us the question is, has marriage to do with well-being or with salvation? Is it a soteriological institution or a welfare institution? Is marriage, this *opus contra naturam*, a path to individuation or a way to well-being?

The following may give us a clue: all marriage ceremonies contain certain religious elements and overtones. A purely civil marriage, so-called, is practically non-existent. The "heathen" inhabitants of Tahiti and the Fiji Islands, who are renowned for their

38

so-called naturalism, allow for a kind of priestly prayer to be sent to the Gods during a wedding ceremony. In the cases of the Yakuts and the Kalmucks a shaman must be present at the wedding. For the ancient Egyptians, marriage rituals were accompanied by certain religious ceremonies. Aeschylus says in the *Orestia* that in marriage husband and wife are bound together by the Gods. Plato asserts that a religious ceremony is necessary to a wedding. For the Hindus, prayers and invocations to the Gods play a large role in the wedding service. Even communistic countries attempt to lend a certain splendor and solemnity to weddings through the use of pseudo-religious ceremonies. There the civil officials try to avoid the impression that a wedding is simply the signing of a contract.

One may object that in most cultures a great many human undertakings are accompanied by some kind of religious ceremony, such as merely eating, hunting, embarking in a ship, etc. Nevertheless, it is noteworthy that not much in the course of life is as surrounded by religious ceremonies as is marriage; only birth and death are taken with equal seriousness. To be sure, one often comes up against resistance to the religious tone of wedding services. Since everyone is supposed to find blessedness in his own fashion, the insistence on connecting human actions and specific soterific ceremonies has to run into rejection.

Certain Buddhists, for example, understand the religious ceremonies of marriage as nothing but a concession to human weakness. Actually, they believe, marriage is only a civil agreement. In the late Roman Empire, marriage was progressively stripped of any religious meaning and moved toward becoming a purely contractual agreement. Religious ceremonies came to be looked upon as practices to ensure the preservation of local color. In the Talmud there are passages that state that marriage is not a religious covenant. Luther pronounced marriage to be the concern of jurists, not of the Church.

Contrary to these pronouncements, however, the Buddhists accompany weddings with many religious rituals, the Jews have in the course of their long history bound religious ceremonies to their weddings, and Luther said: "Over marriage, God has placed a cross."

Zwingli's reformation in Zürich also attempted to design the marriage vows as purely secularly as possible, but the pressure of the people forced the wedding service back again into a religious ceremony.

The character of marriage in Puritan Scotland was given an extremely secular tone. Until 1856 all that was necessary for a marriage in Scotland was the declaration of intention on the part of both partners; every kind of ceremony was avoided.

The Catholic Church did not decide that marriage is valid only with the Church's blessing until the Council of Trent in 1653. Today the Catholic Church views marriage as a sacrament, as a symbol of the marriage of Christ with the Church.

In 1791 France introduced the purely secular marriage. "The law considers marriage a civil contract," was the way it was put. The civil marriage service, however, was designed to include great solemnity, as it is today in East Germany. The civil officer wears a silk sash around his midriff and imitates the gestures of a minister. A civil marriage service in France is often more solemn than a church wedding in Zürich.

Is the presence of references to transcendence in most marriage ceremonies—and that even against great resistance—perhaps an indication that marriage has much more to do with salvation than with well-being? Is this why marriage is a kind of difficult "unnatural institution"?

The life-long dialectical encounter between two partners, the bond of man and woman until death, can be understood as a special path for discovering the soul, as a special form of individuation. One of the essential features of this soteriological pathway is the absence of avenues for escape. Just as the saintly hermits cannot evade themselves, so the married persons cannot avoid their partners. In this partially uplifting, partially tormenting evasionlessness lies the specific character of this path.

In the Christian conception of salvation, love plays an important role. One may wonder perhaps why I have until now only alluded to love in connection with marriage.

The word love includes a great diversity of phenomena, which perhaps have the same source but must nevertheless be distinguished from one another. Marriage is one of the soteriological pathways of love, but of a love that is not altogether identical with what is produced by the wanton youth Cupid. Cupid's love is not to be counted on, is moody, unrestricted. The peculiarity of the love that marks the soteriological pathway of marriage is its "anti-natural" stability: "For better or for worse, for richer or for poorer, in sickness and in health, until death do us part." One frequently sees aged married couples in which one partner is spiritually and physically robust while the other is physically ill and spiritually reduced. And still they love one another, and that not out of compassion or protectiveness. Such cases demonstrate the anti-naturalism and greatness of this kind of love which the soteriological pathway of marriage requires. The love on which marriage rests transcends the "personal relationship" and is more than merely relational.

Everyone has to search for his own soteriological pathway. A painter finds it in painting, an engineer in building, etc. Often people set out on a pathway which later proves not to be the one for them. Many have believed themselves to be artists and later found out that their vocation lay elsewhere.

Is marriage, then, a pathway to salvation for everyone? Are there not people whose psychological development is not furthered by marriage? We do not require that everyone find his salvation in music, for example. Is it not then equally questionable that many think they must find their salvation in marriage? Here one can make the following objection: to be sure there are numerous soteriological pathways, but this fact does not apply to marriage; it occurs to no one that the majority of the population should become painters, but it is expected that a normal person will marry after a certain age. Not to marry, it is supposed, is abnormal. Older people who are single are described as infantile problematical developments: older unmarried men are suspected of homosexuality, and women who have not married are thought to be in this position because of a lack of attractiveness ("The poor thing couldn't find a man."). There exists a virtual terror about everyone's having to marry. Perhaps in this attitude lies one of the biggest problems with respect to modern marriage.

The soteriological character of marriage is becoming ever more important in our time: marriage is becoming ever more a pathway to salvation and ever less an institution of well-being, ever more a vocation. Not everyone believes they have to find their salvation in playing the violin, so why do so many believe themselves to be called to marriage? Such a dominance of one soteriological pathway is destructive. Innumerable people are married today who have no business in marriage.

Despite many modern movements to the contrary, marriage, from the purely social point of view, remains more highly prized than the situation of being single. This was not always the case. In the Middle Ages, for example, the unmarried state was highly regarded. The vocation of nun or priest was approvingly regarded as a soteriological possibility. Singleness on the part of women was closely connected to asexuality, while society was much more tolerant towards men, and sexual acting-out was rarely looked upon as evil for single men.

It is high time to promote the possiblities of the unmarried life for people who seek their salvation elsewhere than in marriage. This would also function to make marriage more valuable. The social position and the material security of single people must be improved, and it should become possible and acceptable for people to have children outside of marriage. The goal would be to reserve marriage only for those people who are especially gifted in finding their salvation in the intensive, *continuous* relationship and dialectical encounter between man and woman.

There are many women, for example, who basically want only children and not a man. For these it is a tragedy that they have to drag a man around with them for a whole lifetime when he does not interest them in the least.

The modern marriage is possible only when this special soteriological pathway is desired and wished for. The collective, however, continues to herd people toward marrying for the sake of well-being. Many girls marry to evade the pressure of a career and to find someone who will take care of them. Only a few marriages

43

can last "until death" if marriage is understood as a welfare institution.

As I mentioned, there are today many counter-movements afoot: women's liberation, for example, would free the woman of the terrifying demand to marry. "Women do not need men," is one of their slogans. Unfortunately, however, women's lib is—or was—often hostile to men.

According to recent statistics, marriage in Western countries is taking place less frequently or taking place later in life. Perhaps a new development is preparing the way for marriage to become a vocation for some and not a duty for all. Many young people are living together without marrying, and perhaps this reflects an acknowledgment that marriage is not *the* pathway to salvation for all. Whether or not this is really indicative of a newly emerging conception of marriage cannot yet be clearly determined. It could also be the expression of a collective pessimism, a loss of belief in any kind of soteriological pathway.

Here we must delve into further difficulties of the modern marriage. As I stressed before, the modern marriage is above all a soteriological pathway and not a welfare institution. But people are continually being taught by psychiatrists, psychologists, marriage counselors, etc., that only happy marriages are good marriages, or that marriages *should* be happy. In fact, however, every path to salvation leads through Hell. Happiness in the sense that it is presented to married couples today belongs to well-being, not to salvation. Marriage above all is a soteriological institution, and this is why it is so filled with highs and lows; it consists of sacrifices, joys, *and* suffering. For instance, a married person may bump up against the psychopathic side of his partner, namely that part of his partner's character which is not amenable to change and which has tormenting consequences for both of them; if the marriage is not to break up at this point, one partner (usually the less psychopathic one) is going to have to give in. Should one of them be emotionally cold, for example, there is no alternative except for the other to continue to show loving feelings, even if the partner reacts to these weakly and inadequately. All of the well-intentioned advice to men and women in the vein of "That just won't do," or "You must not tolerate that," or "A man (or woman) must not let that happen to himself," are therefore false and deleterious.

A marriage only works if one opens himself to exactly that which he would never ask for otherwise. Only through rubbing oneself sore and losing oneself is one able to learn about oneself, God, and the world. Like every soteriological pathway, that of marriage is hard and painful.

A writer who creates meaningful works does not want to become happy, he wants to be creative. Likewise married people can seldom enjoy happy, harmonious marriages, as psychologists would force it upon them and lead them to believe. The image of the "happy marriage" causes great damage.

For those who are gifted for the soteriological pathway of marriage, it, like every such pathway, naturally offers not only trouble, work, and suffering, but the deepest kind of existential satisfaction. Dante did not get to Heaven without traversing Hell. And so also there seldom exist "happy marriages."

MASCULINE AND FEMININE
DO NOT HARMONIZE

To understand modern marriage more fully we need to reflect further on the masculine-feminine phenomenon and on the relationship between man and woman. What are we, actually, as men, women, persons? What determines our everyday behavior? I will try to limit myself to only a few viewpoints that are important to our theme.

The activities of animals are determined in part by inborn patterns of behavior. Outer stimuli provoke or release certain inborn patterns of behavior. As a rule, these inherited patterns of behavior are adequate to and useful in the situation that is characterized by particular stimuli. The life of the species and of the individual is maintained by the full execution of this pattern of behavior.

In the spring, for example, certain stimuli cause some species of birds to build nests according to an absolutely specific design. As soon as the eggs are hatched and the parents see the open mouths of the young, the behavioral pattern of feeding is activated. Artificial devices can be substituted for natural stimuli and the same effect is achieved. A male bird will perform a particular courting ritual if a female appears. But the female is recognized by him only as a thing that is characterized by a particular form and color or perhaps by a certain sound; this sound alone can be enough to release the behavioral pattern of mating. This is true not only of birds, as illustrated by the following story.

In Canada it was observed that during the rutting season

male elk would throw themselves headlong against moving trains. It was then discovered that the whistle of the locomotive resembled the roaring of a male elk in rut, and this was why there occurred a "duel" between elk and locomotive. Such behavior certainly not the result of any sort of reflection. The animal reacts "instinctively", not in the sense of a vague, indefinite urge, but in the sense of bringing to completion exactly regulated patterns of behavior which usually are meaningful in relation to the given situation.

Humans are different, though not completely so. We too carry within us inherent ways of behaving, which are called archetypes. The difference between human archetypal patterns and the inborn patterns of reaction and behavior in animals is as follows:

The patterns of behavior among humans are, first of all, usually more complicated and less precise in detail than are those of animals. Human patterns of behavior have to do with general guidelines that work in the background of actual behavior. Secondly, human patterns of behavior seem to be more numerous and are not all utilized in the course of a lifetime; many of them simply lie fallow. Every person has a great many potential patterns of behavior within him that play hardly any role at all in his uniquely specific life. Thirdly, and this of the most decisive importance, the human being is capable of observing these patterns of behavior and of reflecting on them: he is able now and again to bring these archetypes into consciousness. But this occurs usually not through logical thinking and reflection but through images, symbols, myths, stories, etc. Man is an animal who becomes aware through symbols.

All of this must be more or less familiar to the reader. Despite this, however, a certain amount of confusion and obfuscation reigns in regard to the question of masculine and feminine. It should be clear that there is not only *one* masculine archetype and *one* feminine archetype. There are dozens, if not hundreds, of feminine and masculine archetypes. Certainly there are many more of them than we usually imagine. But not all archetypes are dominant at a particular period in the life of an individual. Moreover, every historical epoch has its dominant masculine and feminine archetypes. Women and men are determined in their sexual identities and behavior by only a select number of archetypes. Behavior is determined only by those patterns that are momentarily dominant in the collective psyche. This leads to a grotesque but understandable error: the archetypes that dominate masculine and feminine behavior in a particular time come to be understood as *the* masculine and feminine archetypes. And from this limited number of archetypes it is decided what "masculinity" and "femininity" are. This misunderstanding has led, for example, to the assumption in Jungian psychology that masculinity is identical with Logos, and femininity with Eros. It is assumed that the essence of femininity is personal, related to one's fellow man, passive, masochistic, and that the essence of masculinity is abstract, intellectual, aggressive, sadistic, active, etc. This naive assertion could have been made only because the masculine and feminine archetypes that were dominant at that time and in that culture were understood as the only valid ones.

I would like to mention here just a few of the numerous feminine archetypes.

First there is the maternal archetype: in its chthonic form nourishing and protective on the one side, devouring on the other;

in its spiritual form inspiring on the one side, impelling towards madness and death on the other.

A somewhat more dismal archetype is symbolized in the *mater dolorosa*, depicted in thousands of paintings and sculptures. It is the woman who has lost her son, whose son has been killed in the war or has died in an accident in his youth, the mother of the fallen airplane pilot. Such a mother often identifies herself so strongly with the archetype of the *mater dolorosa* that she seems to herself to have become another woman since her loss.

The archetype of Hera, wife of the heavenly father Zeus, is familiar to us as the symbol of the jealous wife, fierce and terrible towards everything that diverts her husband's attention from herself.

Another archetype is the *hetaera*, the uninhibited companion of men in sexual pleasure, in wit, and in learning. Today we may experience this archetype, for example, in the actress Shirley MacLaine: intellectual, independent, but not hostile to men.

Another feminine archetype is presented in Aphrodite, the Goddess of sexual pleasure, the archetype of the desirable beloved; this archetype was seen, for instance, in the childish, untutored Brigitte Bardot, and in a different way, in Marilyn Monroe.

Athene presents a most interesting feminine archetype: the wise, energetic woman, self-sufficient, non-sexual, nevertheless helpful to men, played and lived out a few years ago by Eleanor Roosevelt.

Certain widows and divorced women often seem to have something archetypal about them. They are independent, the man is absent, and one gets the impression of "thank God!" The relation to the lost husband is that of conqueror to conquered.

Masculine and Feminine

These archetypes are all more or less related to the male, whether as husband or lover, and to children or to the family. Were these the only feminine archetypes, one could rightfully conclude that feminine nature is characterized by Eros, by relatedness.

Feminine archetypes that have nothing to do with men—at least with man as husband or lover—or with children are just as important as the above, though less familiar to the collective consciousness.

There is, for instance, the archetype of the Amazon, the female warrior. She needs men only to procreate children. According to some reports, the Amazons captured men and slept with them in order to become pregnant; once the men had fulfilled their function they were killed. According to another version, the Amazons used men not only to engender children but also to do the household chores, to cook and to rear the children. Amazons love conquests, and they feel good in the company of other women. This is the archetype of the independent career woman who rejects men. We also know of an archetype of the solitary Amazon, an older or younger woman who loves to travel about by herself, visiting people, who however does not want to attach herself to anything, who views men with distrust, who feels comfortable with women but is not lesbian.

Another feminine archetype is that of Artemis. Her disposition toward men, too, is hostile. She does not want to be seen or known by them. Men who accidentally stumble upon her must die. If Artemis has a relation to anyone, it is to her brother Apollo. Many women are in this same way affectively related only to their brothers; outside of that they want to have nothing whatever to do with men or with children. This can be understood not only as the result of a neurotic development, but also as the enactment of one archetypal possibility of the feminine.

Another archetype that is not related to men or children is that of the Vestal Virgin, the nun or priestess. These women give their lives to God or sacrifice it to something else, but not to a man or to children.

We can conclude that there are just as many feminine archetypes that are not related to husband, lover, or children, as there are of those which serve the Eros of sexuality and family life.

A more exact study of the archetypal possiblities of human beings could contribute much to the understanding of the so-called neuroses. A too limited vision of what man should be hinders us from understanding the countless possible archetypal variations of human behavior. Many of the so-called neurotically false attitudes are not the result of an unfavorable psychological development, as we usually understand them, but the image of a particular archetype which cannot be lived with a good conscience because it is rejected by the collective. Practically whole archetypal patterns of feminine behavior which do not relate to men are relegated to "should not be," and are seen as neurotic and sick. It need not necessarily be neurotic if husband or child do not stand in the center of a woman's interest. The Amazon, Artemis, the Vestal Virgin, etc., are possible feminine patterns of behavior, grounded in archetypes and not necessarily in psychopathology.

Archetypes need certain circumstances and spiritual movements in a particular historical period in order to be activated and lived. Thus there have been times and situations in which the archetype of the artist was not highly valued; in times of peace the archetype of the warrior has played no important role, etc.

Masculine and Feminine

A most dominant feminine archetype has been that of the mother; in almost all historical periods this has been vigorously lived out and has dominated the behavior of most women. Children need mothers; without them, mankind would die out.

What is the archetypal situation for women today? Which archetypes dominate? Which have lost some of their meaning? Noteworthy in western Europe is the decline of the dominance of the maternal archetype in the last ten to fifteen years. I would surmise that in many historical "high" cultures this archetype lost much of its meaning for particular social classes, e.g., among the higher social classes of the Roman Empire, among French nobility of the eighteenth century, etc.

In this connection we have today in western Europe and in several other industrial areas of the world a very interesting situation. When children come into the world they have a good chance of living for seventy years. In earlier periods only a few children reached adulthood, so it was necessary for the survival of humanity that the available women bore as many children as possible. Even those who reached adulthood often died early. This means that most women died before they ever reached an age where the mother archetype was no longer a necessity. Today, however, the average woman in western Europe bears perhaps two or three children, who, after she has reached the age of forty-five or so, no longer demand all her energy.

Earlier it was possible only for the very wealthy, who had the benefit of maids and servants, to not lose most of their psychological energy in caring for children. Nowadays servants and maids are rare even among the wealthy, but in exchange for this (at least in Western Europe) the women of all classes have fewer household

52

chores thanks to the improvement of household technology. Also the care of small children today requires less trouble and effort.

Since the mother archetype and the Hera archetype are less dominant today, more room is left for other archetypes to emerge. Numerous other archetypes contain psychic energy. The contemporary woman has the opportunity to live into the most diverse archetypes.

Significantly, the situation for men is not precisely the same. For them not much has changed. For millenia men have had more archetypal possibilities than women have had. The archetype of Ares, the simple, brutal warrior and soldier, has always been available to them, and so has that of Odysseus, the clever warrior and husband. The archetype of the priest, the man of God, has always been viable for men. The archetype of the medicine man, the doctor, that of Hephaistos the clever technician, that of Hermes the clever trader and thief, and many others were not closed to men. The fact that today's woman has more archetypal possibilities open to her does not mean automatically that today's man also has more possibilities at his disposal than in the past. The man of today is still very much bound to his role as provider, and this limits his possibilities. The archetypal possibilities for men are not much more numerous than those for women, but for women this great opportunity is somewhat novel. For this reason I am dealing more with feminine than with masculine archetypes.

Women, who until now could only enact a few archetypes and make them definite in their behavior, are becoming increasingly stirred up by the opening of new possibilities. Unfortunately a very unhappy, difficult complication is now showing its face, a complication that we will want to explore a bit. The passage over from one archetype to another, or the awakening of a new one that has been heretofore neglected, is a situation that is always fraught with difficulty. We know of such passages in every life history. During puberty the archetype of the child recedes into the background, and the archetype of the adult emerges. Around the age of fifty the latter one slowly begins to be suppressed by the *senex* archetype. When one archetype becomes detached from another, we find in the life of the individual the so-called transition depressions; these are the well-known depressions that occur during puberty and during the period between forty-five and fifty-five. This kind of depression in an individual's life history can be mastered and overcome, for we know precisely which archetype is becoming detached.

The difficult collective situation of women today cannot, however, be seen as simply parallel to an individual's transition depression.

To illuminate this further let me offer a few brief psychological reflections. Everything that we are, we are through the working out, through the experience and the refinement and the humanization, of the archetype. Precise archetypal patterns always govern our behavior. We can cultivate this behavior, grasp it in images, become conscious of it, and give form to it. But we can seldom function solely from the will in important matters. To say this another way, we experience our activity as meaningful only when it is related to an archetypal foundation. A mother can never function with satisfaction as a mother, if her mothering is done only out of conscious reflection or only from an ego intention and feeling. She cannot have a merely personal relationship to the child. Her relationship to the child is fundamentally impersonal and

54

archetypal. It has to do with the archetype of "mother and child," and only on this archetypal ground can a personal relationship of "mother-child" be built up.

Moreover, we are unable to choose an archetype by an act of conscious decision. The archetype is given to us through the workings of an outer situation and the collective unconscious. Those archetypes that rule in the collective rule also in us. Which collective archetypes are dominant is shown in the dominant images, myths, and figures of film, advertising, popular stories, etc. Here are a few examples: Elizabeth II, symbol of the archetype of the queen and wife; Jacqueline Kennedy, the one who achieves fame and riches through men; ex-empress Soraya, the woman of free love; Elizabeth Taylor, the man-consuming beauty; James Bond, the adventurer who masters technology and exhausts women; the orgiastic rock singers, like Dionysos nearly torn to pieces by their female followers; the trickster-like Mickey Mouse; the hero Muhammed Ali, whose braggadocio before battle is Homeric.

The situation of women today is especially hazardous because they are detaching themselves from a small group of archetypes and approaching a larger group of them, but the new group is not yet clearly visible. In this sense their situation is different from that of an individual's transition depression. The situation today is that women are somewhat at sea: the old continent disappears, the new one has not yet become completely visible. Such a passage brings with it an archetypal emptiness. Lost, searching, helpless, the ship of womanhood floats on the wide ocean. And this archetypal transition situation is also one of the reasons why so many women want to find *themselves* and have the wish to be themselves, to live only their *own* lives. Again and again women come to psychologists, counselors, or psychiatrists, saying that they are unhappy and would like for once to live only their own lives, to be themselves or to find themselves. The so-called self-discovery of women over forty is today a favorite topic of women's magazines and of popular psychological articles.

This "being oneself" is of course impossible. All the talk about it is the expression of a collective lostness, confusion and depression. To say, "I want to be only myself" makes about as much sense as saying, "I want to speak my own language." One has to express himself in the language he has grown up with from childhood or has learned since then. One cannot speak his "own" language, and moreover, even if one did, no one else could understand it. Similarly, we cannot find ourselves but can only express ourselves through archetypal role enactments, and in this way we may also—perhaps—find ourselves.

There can be no doubt that a new freedom will constellate itself for the modern woman. Even today a woman is partially in a situation where she can allow herself to be engaged by more archetypal roles than was formerly the case. She can be mother, beloved, companion, Amazon, Athene, etc.

I would not venture at the present time to abstract "the feminine" from all the known feminine archetypes, or "the masculine" from the masculine archetypes. This would require, for one thing, female psychologists who would not just continue to study the subject through masculine lenses like good pupils of the master. Nevertheless, one thing is certain: we must put an end to the equations, "feminine = Eros and relatedness" and "masculine = Logos, intellect, activity." (Athene, for example, presents a feminine form of intellectuality that cannot be understood as "animus.") And end

56

must also be made to the biological view that a woman fulfills herself only in child-rearing.

The many new archetypal possibilities now on the horizon have a further interesting consequence: fear of the multiplicity of archetypal possibilities. Women are accustomed to being conditioned and led by only a few archetypes. The new multiplicity that is emerging is making many women feel insecure; they feel themselves driven to hold on to the *fewest* possible archetypes. For centuries the archetype of Hera has dominated women. Today the archetype of the professional woman is beginning its one-sided domination. Women suffer from the collective compulsion to go to work as soon as the mother-archetype has run its course. Instead of freely giving themselves to the multiplicity of archetypal possibilities, they often surrender to the image of the professional woman and believe they find "fulfillment" even in the most boring positions, to which they have often given themselves without the slightest economic necessity. Not a few married women in their fifties who have become free of the burden of small children have compulsively sacrificed their freedom to a tiresome, subservient professional position. The professional-woman archetype is closely bound up with the technical, rational, utilitarian "Gods" of our times. One often hears, "I would like to do something useful."

Should the whole range of the new archetypal spectrum actually break through, however, the relationship between men and women will be re-formed in many new ways.

Many new and extremely diverse relationships between man and woman will be enacted: Hera-Zeus, power-addicted wife and brutal husband; Philemon—Baucis, the affectionate , faithful couple; Ares-Aphrodite, a relationship between the sensuous woman

57

who is amazed at brutality, and the ruffian who worships beauty; Zeus and the nymphs, the detached man in love with sexual intoxication, relating to numerous women friends; Aphrodite and her countless lovers, etc.

Zeus and Hera are to be understood as the President and First Lady of Olympus. But their prominence will diminish, and this will make room for uncounted new Gods and Goddesses to appear and develop. In spite of this, Zeus and Hera will remain very highly regarded.

Archetypes that until now have been exiled to the underworld of pathology can be lived out more intensely. The relationship of Odysseus to Athene will no longer be pathologized into a mother complex; men will be able to relate to women in an asexual manner; the archetype of the siblings will again be able to be lived out—the Artemis-Apollo relationship—and the intimate, persistent, all-encompassing love between brother and sister will no longer be condemned as incest or unhealthy bond. (Interestingly enough, this sibling relationship was less pathologized and less understood as 'incest' in Queen Victoria's time than it is today.) Also appearing, though, will be militant, man-hating feminine archetypes, and the Amazons will win recognition. There will be women who will openly express their wish to be only mothers, not wives. Feminine archetypes will be enacted that have nothing whatever to do with one's fellowmen, but are oriented only to a profession: women scientists, artists, etc.

All of this is music of the future. At the present time, women, and the relations between women and men, are in a transitional phase. The uncertainty inherent in this situation frightens us, not only because we do not know which archetypes are going to come up, but also because in such times of transition we are much more open both to the splendor of the archetypes and to their sinister and disturbing daimonism. To reflect on this and to hold it before our eyes is extraordinarily difficult and frightens us to the depths. Humanity has always sought for ways to render this situation innocuous as soon as it came to consciousness. Herein lies a trap for those who think to obtain a trustworthy image of the archetypes from a traditional mythology, such as that of the Greeks. Mythologies, fairy tales, etc., are often full of sharply delineated archetypal symbols, but often they are also made up of a mixture of depotentiated, aestheticized, and moralized images.

In recent times psychology has begun to recognize the destructive daimonism of the maternal and paternal archetypes. Kronos, who devours his children, and the Mother-Goddess, who demands human sacrifice, appear once again in the knowledge that much neurotic suffering is occasioned through the destructiveness of parents. "Mommy and Daddy" are no longer presented as so completely harmless, and suddenly they even seem to be to blame for everything!

Unfortunately, psychology has not yet arrived at a similar conclusion with respect to the relationship between man and woman. We have identified the aggressive with the masculine, but we have all too often seen the feminine coupled with unaggressive Eros. We still, even in the twentieth century, do not want to look squarely at the archetype of the feminine that ruins a man's life and kills him.

We speak of the *femme fatale* and of *la belle dame sans merci*. Marlene Dietrich sang, "Men swarm about me like moths to the light—and burn up." Psychologically, however, these figures are not taken seriously in the archetypal sense. Within the realm of archetypal possibilities, the relations between man and woman are not limited to either vital relationships or mutual independence of one another; they also include mutual strife and battle against one another, mutual rejection, Amazonian hatred for men, the anger of fanatical women's lib, the ham-fisted brutality of Zeus, and the malevolent contrariness of Hera. The destructive and aggressive side of a man's relation to woman has been progressively acknowledged, but the death-lust of woman against man has been either unrecognized or pathologized because of a one-sided understanding of the feminine.

The archetypal images of feminine, man-killing aggressivity in the mythological figures of Penthesilea, Camilla, Juturna, Marfisa, Bradamanta, Clorinda, Britomart, Belphoebe, Radigund are misunderstood as unfeminine, as imitative of masculinity, or as androgenous. The militant, man-killing woman who, dressed in heavy armor, knocks one man after the other out of the saddle is not in the least bit unfeminine; rather, she presents us with a feminine archetype that for hundreds, even for thousands, of years has been "out of fashion."

The recognition of primary feminine murderous aggressivity will bring a colossal enrichment of conscious experiential possibilities to mankind on the one hand, but countless complications on the other. Strindberg recognized these possibilities of the feminine but did not enlarge on them because of the intention to present the woman-annihilating masculine archetype. Was it because of this that he got "pathologized" as a woman-hater?

For a further understanding of marriage it is very important to realize not only that masculine and feminine can relate to one another through hostility, but that they don't even have to be "relating" at all. There are many archetypally feminine ways of relating in which a man plays no part whatsoever, and many archetypally masculine ways which have no connection to the feminine. Man and woman, therefore, complement one another only partially. Marriage can be really understood properly only when we free ourselves from the "harmony complex."

When men and women jostle one another it must, on archetypal grounds, result in heavy conflict and misunderstanding. And when men and women draw *toward* each other, there may be more than "loving" afoot; rejecting and annihilating may also play a part. The partners may not be at all attracted to each other; they don't even complement or understand one another in their acts of rejection or aggressiveness. A marriage may well be built around existential solitariness, which had not been recognized for what it was. All these unharmonious factors do not always have to do with a neurotic development or a neurotic relationship.

Marriage is not comfortable and harmonious; rather, it is a place of individuation where a person rubs up against himself and against his partner, bumps up against him in love and in rejection, and in this fashion learns to know himself, the world, good and evil, the heights and the depths.

AN EXAMPLE OF
AN INDIVIDUATION MARRIAGE

And yet: Somehow many marriages last until death. As we shall see, without sacrifice marriage seldom works. The sacrifice in individuation often takes strange forms; but only individuation makes marriage intelligible.

In the following, the presentation of a case is given as an illustration and as a stimulus for further investigation. I am fully conscious of the problem inherent in a case presentation, namely, that the case is chosen as a rule to prove what one wants to prove.

I have received the approval of the person involved to publicize her story as a case study. I have changed some of the details of her identity, and so I present her in the light of this other, somewhat foreign identity. The members of the family have assured me that they do not believe they will be recognized, and have further assured me that if they are it will not disturb them.

The case, then. He is a small, somewhat unattractive, intelligent businessman without any academic education. She is a good-looking woman, of average intelligence, with an academic background in the humanities. They are of about the same age. They met each other when they were twenty-five years old. They quickly fell in love, and she became pregnant. The marriage followed, not actually under the pressure of the pregnancy, but because they both loved each other ardently.

The wife admired the husband for his business acumen, his independence, and his determination to succeed. He prized her physical beauty and her academic learning, her culture.

After the marriage the husband began a business and had at first to occupy himself a good deal with its growth. He had to work hard, often late into the night. She introduced him somewhat into the realms of what one calls "culture," and continued to admire his abilities as a businessman.

After their second child she began to interest herself exclusively in the children; increasingly she shut herself off from her husband. In the private conversations between them she made use of her academic learning. He became very servile and tried to make life as comfortable as possible for his wife, helped her with the housework, etc. He began, however, to feel a profound resentment against his wife. When he came home one night slightly intoxicated and his wife asked him to help her with some household chores, he exploded, and after some arguing slapped her face. Both of them were terribly frightened by this and turned to a marriage counselor for help.

The marriage counselor spoke with them separately. He told the wife that for neurotic reasons she was trying to control her husband too much. He advised her to be kinder to him and to respect him more. In addition, he attempted to get the wife to experience anew her recently diminished admiration for the business qualities of her husband. To the husband the marriage counselor explained that for neurotic reasons he was not strong and independent enough in his dealings with his wife. He warned him about his drinking and advised him in no uncertain terms not to strike his wife again. He saw that the husband was full of suppressed aggression, and advised him on this account to go into analysis.

An Individuation Marriage

Among other things the analysis showed that the husband basically understood more about "culture" than did his wife. For example, he took great pleasure in literature and painting. He became more self-confident, but his wife could not tolerate his new attitude. She was used to having him give in to her. After a vigorous confrontation between them, she left with the two children and took refuge with her mother. She then sought the advice of another counselor who was unknown to her husband. The counselor accepted the portrait of the husband which she painted, namely, that he was a very industrious, uneducated, emotionally rigid, insensitive and uptight self-made man. The two of them concluded that it would be difficult to change the husband, and in the event that the marriage could be saved at all, it would have to be at the cost of her playing the obedient housewife.

After several weeks the husband appeared at the home of the mother-in-law and took his wife and children back home with him. Both spouses agreed that, all things considered, it was worth it to continue the marriage. He became softer, and gave up the hope of ever being able to really establish his own position *vis-à-vis* his wife. He praised her academic qualities frequently, and in the presence of friends he often quoted the opinions of his wife on cultural matters in order to please her. In the household he helped her wherever he could, even when he was overworked in his business. For her part, she hardly took any notice of his business problems. Often it would happen that when he came home from work, dead tired, and longed for nothing more than settling into an easy chair and watching TV for awhile, he would have to go to the theater with her. She controlled him completely.

In the meantime she had become pretty cool sexually. She

could reach orgasm only when the husband pretended to pay her by placing a one hundred franc note on the night-table. In day-dreams she loved to see herself as a prostitute in a bordello.

In sexual matters the husband had some masochistic tendencies. He could come to ejaculation only if during intercourse she would pull his hair. They told each other their sexual fantasies. Communications between them never broke down completely; there would always be days when they could speak together very well.

The husband at one point had the following dream. He saw the familiar picture in which Aristotle is kneeling on the floor while a woman is riding on top of him. But in this case he himself was Aristotle, and his own wife was riding on him. In the dream he saw further that his wife had mutilated legs and therefore could not walk.

The dream can be interpreted from many angles. For us it shows the following: the man is being dominated by his wife; she, however, is unable to walk on her own legs. For this reason she has no choice other than to "ride" him. Granted, it has to do here with a "neurotic" marriage: he is somewhat masochistic, while she compensates his basically materialistic, "raw" side through a so-called interest in culture. Moreover, the wife obviously is at bottom completely dependent; she can function, therefore, only if she can find someone who enjoys being controlled, and only through such a situation is she helped to some degree of independence.

I will not here pursue the subjective meaning of the dream, in which the wife represents the anima of the dreamer.

The husband had a recurrent dream which appeared especially

frequently after he had had a heavy encounter with his wife. In a small dark room he saw a man playing the piano; often he himself was this man. The dream figure always had to play some kind of melody: he had no other choice than to sit in this room and try to play a particular melody.

Once he dreamed that he saw the notes which he (or the man) was supposed to play. The melody chosen was called *Le Marriage.*

To the small dark room the patient associated the small room in the house of his parents in which, as a boy, he liked to spend time in thought and reflection. Moreover, it was there that he had first discovered that he could think, that he was capable of reflecting on himself and on others.

The man was utterly unmusical, but he remembered that as a boy he had liked to listen to organ music and had enjoyed singing along in church. Even now church music had something compelling in it for him. For him music was somehow associated with that which cannot be understood, with the divine.

This dream is to be understood in part as a compulsive individuation dream. *Le Marriage* was the melody that he had to play and that brought him nearer to the divine, that helped him therefore to individuate.

Granted, the dream of the man was peculiar, but it compelled him from within to play the melody *Le Marriage,* the melody of marriage.

The husband had a further interesting association to the dream. He associated it to a juggler of whom he had once read in a novel, and about whom he remembered the following: A medieval town once built a great cathedral dedicated to the glory of God and the

Holy Virgin. In order to prove their reverence, all the inhabitants
contributed a part to the building: the architect donated the plans,
the carpenter constructed the rafters, the mason built the walls,
the painter decorated the interior, the goldsmith fashioned impressive candle-holders, etc. When the construction of the cathedral
was completed, a great festival was celebrated, and everyone felt
God to be very near. Late at night a priest was crossing through
the cathedral to see that everything was in order, and at the altar
he came across a juggler, vigorously pursuing his art with balls
and bats. Full of righteous indignation, the priest launched into
the artist, to which the entertainer replied: "Everyone in this
town has a craft, which each has used for the glory of God in
building this church; I have no skills outside of being able to jug-
gle balls and bats in the air, and that is what I am doing here, for
the glory of God."

The dreamer associated his piano playing to the juggling of
the festival artist.

Certainly we come here upon the question of how far a
marriage partner (in this case the husband) can go in giving in,
time and again, to his spouse, before he does damage not only to
his own individuation but his partner's as well. In this case the
wife could continue to demand more and more.

In answer to this we can only allude here to the fairy tale of
"The Fisherman and His Wife." Owing to the pressure of his wife,
the poor fisherman must keep on asking more and more from the
wonder-working fish.

> Flounder, flounder in the sea,
> Prithee, hearken unto me:
> My wife, Ilsebil, must have her own will,

And sends me to beg a boon of thee.
Finally, at the instigation of his wife, he asks for too much, and
both end up as poor as they were at the start.

SEXUALITY AND REPRODUCTION

Now that we have gone into the subject of marriage and
have taken a look at the relationship between masculine and feminine *per se,* we will approach the subject of sexuality. In marriage,
and in the relationship of man and woman generally, sexuality
plays a decisive role. The word "sexuality" is overused these days
to the point of boredom. It is spoken so often that one comes to
believe that he knows what he is talking about. What sort of psychological phenomenon are we describing with the word sexuality,
or "sex?"

The Greeks of classical times expressed themselves significantly more poetically and more precisely than we do. They spoke of
Aphrodite, born of the foam of the sea, formed out of the severed
genitalia of Ouranos, the sky-God, son of Chaos. She was charming
and seductive. Paris gave the golden apple not to Athene nor to
Hera, but to Aphrodite. She was the wife of the crippled smith,
Hephaistos, but she was fonder of the war-God Ares, who scattered
fear among mankind.

Another Greek mythological figure is *Priapos,* a God of so-
called "fertility." He was represented as an ugly man with gigantic
genitals who boldly swaggers throughout the wide world.

Best known is *Eros.* According to the *Theogeny* of Hesiod, this God has existed since the beginning of time: he was born from Chaos. He was present at the "birth" of Aphrodite. At first he was associated with homoeroticism. In later periods (e.g., in Ovid's time) he was described as a frivolous boy. He traveled through the earth with bow and arrow, some of his arrows having golden tips. If either Gods or men were struck by these, they fell into the madness of love. Others of his arrows had leaden tips, and anyone struck by these became insensitive to love. Still later in history, a company of Eros figures was spoken of, namely, the Erotes. These were tiny winged beings who most suspiciously resembled the creatures who escaped from Pandora's box.

Perhaps it is psychologically more correct and more realistic to speak of numerous differentiated Gods and Goddesses, all of whom are surrounded by stories, than to speak of a *single* entity called sexuality. This is a primitive, limited word that cannot begin to do justice to this multifaceted phenomenon.

Not only the Greeks, but many other peoples as well, have represented sexuality in mythological images. Here is an example from a completely different culture, the Winnebago Indian tribe of North America. In connection with Watjunkaga, a trickster-figure in their mythology, sexuality is described as something completely independent of its bearer. Watjunkaga is an immoral figure who plays pranks and has pranks played upon him. He carries his gigantic male member around with him in a chest, as though it has little to do with him personally. This member swims independently through the water toward bathing girls. The image of this independent, detached sexuality is psychologically very striking. Of course it fits in with the image of man which prevails in the culture of the Winnebago—an image that exhibits significantly fewer centralized characteristics than does ours. Man is understood to consist of several part-souls. Even we contemporary Westerners often express ourselves in similar colloquialisms: we say, for instance, that our "heart hurts," when we actually mean that *we* are feeling hurt, not just our hearts.

Ethnologists describe archaic peoples who see no connection between sexuality and reproduction. They experience these two sets of phenomena as completely separate. Today practically every child knows that sexuality is bound up with the conceiving of the next generation. But were these archaic peoples perhaps more correct from a psychological point of view? What is the connection, actually, between sexuality and reproduction?

It is very striking how in the courses of Jewish and Christian theological history, sexuality and reproduction became forcibly bound to one another. Until recent times, sexuality could be indulged in only in connection with reproduction. St. Paul, for instance, rejected sexuality as such, recognizing it only with certain qualifications if it were sanctified through marriage. He considered it better to marry and to live sexually within marriage than to burn in lustful, unmarital, sexual sinfulness. St. Augustine then specified that sexuality could be recognized as legitimate within marriage because it served the purpose of reproduction. He fundamentally rejected sexual pleasure. St. Thomas, too, and other fathers of the church held the view that sexual pleasure is sinful in every case but could be excused when placed in the service of intramarital reproduction. Albertus Magnus and Duns Scotus then advocated the position that sexual pleasure does not need forgiving when occurring within the context of marriage and serving the purpose of reproduction.

Sexuality and Reproduction

The justification of sexuality by virtue of its reproductive purpose has appeared in modern times, but in secularized versions. Many medical doctors and psychiatrists of the nineteenth century attempted to understand sexuality biologically, from the viewpoint of reproduction. For this reason masturbation, sexual fantasies, and the like were regarded as something unhealthy and disturbing to the nervous system. Until very recently it was common to tell children that masturbation could lead to crippling and to serious disease.

The conceptualizations of nineteenth-century psychiatrists were molded (though not consciously) by Christian opinions. Kraepelin, for instance, was of the opinion that the origin of sexual disorders was almost always masturbation. The fear of masturbation may seem somewhat peculiar today, but it is completely understandable within its historical context. The meaning of sexuality was understood as reproduction, and therefore masturbation was regarded as pathological or sinful since it could never lead to conception. Kraepelin went further, considering that sexual disorders originated in the mental images and fantasies that accompanied masturbation. Sexual fantasies were for him pathological, and this too is understandable given the historical background.

Kraepelin believed that the further sexuality departs from reproduction, the more pathological it becomes.

Officially, nineteenth-century psychiatry was anything but Christian. It is interesting to observe, however, how medieval theological ideas molded even the understanding of human psychopathology. The naive biologism of the nineteenth century, which saw sexuality only in relation to reproduction, obviously had not outgrown the medieval understanding of sexual life. Nevertheless, investigators of this period began to occupy themselves intensively with the subject of sexuality.

There certainly does exist a kind of practical sexuality that is directed only towards reproduction. One finds this among certain hysterical women. The concept of hysteria is not very common anymore and is much argued about. My opinion is that it is still clinically and psychologically very useful. One of the peculiarities of so-called hysterics, which is described by many authors, is the primacy of archaic, primitive ways of relating. For example, we often find among hysterics, be they men or women, a sort of primitive flight-reflex. Under certain conditions these people run screaming in panic away from relationships. A similar form of primitive reaction which overtakes people with hysterical traits is the sudden, complete paralysis in fear-inspiring situations. Is this a relic of the reflex to feign death? When the attacked animal or person no longer stirs or shows any movement, the attacker is no longer aroused and pulls back from his victim.

Another archaic mode of reaction is the sensitivity of the hysterical person to all sorts of non-verbal communication. Hysterics often sense what is going on in the other person before he senses it himself. With hysterics the ability to communicate directly with the souls of others, without the use of speech or any other obvious form of expression, still seems to be strongly developed. Put another way: this archaic ability has not been disturbed by a strong ego development.

The sexuality of hysterical women shows some very interesting characteristics in this connection. Many women with an hysterical character are completely cold sexually when it comes to the actual sexual act, and are unable to reach orgasm. On the other hand, these women are often very coquettish and active in seduction and foreplay. They are gifted for the attraction and sexualization of the man. At the moment of sexual union, however, they feel very little.

This kind of "hysterical sexuality" can be understood as archaic sexuality. What is important for the conception of children is only that the man be excited to sexual activity. Once things have progressed to this point it would be, for the purposes of reproduction, only a waste of energy for the woman, who has reached the point of union, to then experience anything special. Orgasm is not biologically necessary; fertilization can take place without it.

One also finds such primitive sexuality among men. There are undifferentiated men for whom the only important thing is to reach ejaculation, no matter how or where. Any sort of foreplay or afterplay is uninteresting or unintelligible for them. Such an archaic sexuality, which primarily works in the service of reproduction, is often found among men and women who, for one reason or another, were culturally deprived and were not allowed to experience any sort of psychic stimulation during childhood.

It is remarkable that it was precisely this animalistic, primitive sexuality which was for so long understood by Christian theologians to be the only kind without sin, as long as it was sanctified by marriage and served reproduction.

Christianity, however, is only the heir of conceptions that were important in the Old Testament. The purposeless loss of the male's semen counted in the Old Testament as a serious crime against God.

Just how repulsive and animalistic this teaching is—that sexuality must justify itself through reproduction—is demonstrated when one takes it seriously. It would mean, in practice, that only a completely insensitive, biologically-oriented copulation could be considered good. It would be equivalent to saying that eating is not sinful only if one devours the simplest food with one's hands as quickly as possible and without any cultivation, simply for the satiation of appetite.

One certainly has the right to question whether the basis of sexuality is reproduction. Very little of the time and energy that people give to sexuality has anything to do with begetting children. Sexual life begins in earliest childhood and ends only at the grave. By sexual life I understand sexual fantasies, masturbation and sexual play, as well as the actual sexual act. Only a very small portion of sexual life is expressed in deeds. The greatest part consists of fantasies and dreams. That these have but little to do with reproduction is obvious. What we too seldom realize, however, is that even most sexual deeds have little if anything to do with reproduction. This is not only because we have better contraceptives. Most sexual activities have always been without biological usefulness. Although sexuality has always been bound up with reproduction, this alone does not make it intelligible.

The connection of sexuality with reproduction has greatly cramped sexuality. Consciously or not, "normal sexuality" is still more or less understood as a sexuality which derives its norms from the goal of reproduction. Even today many psychologists regard any form of sexual activity which has no clear connection with fertilization as abnormal.

The teaching of the Catholic Church—one-sidedly understood to be sure—has done much harm in this respect. In the nineteenth century, Catholic thinking bound itself closely to biologism. This resulted in the popular Catholic view that a) sexuality should be experienced only within marriage, b) sexuality should be experienced only with a view to reproduction, and c) the purpose of marriage lay above all in the production and rearing of children. The *finis primarius* of marriage is reproduction and child-rearing, while on the other hand St. Augustine had said: *"in nostrarum quippe nuntilis plus valet sanctitas sacramenti quam fecunditas uteri"* ("the sacrament is more important than the fruitfulness of the mother").

THE NONSENSE OF "NORMAL" SEXUALITY

A decisive breakthrough in the understanding of sexual life was made by Freud. In our day the understanding of sexuality is unthinkable apart from a precise knowledge of his theories on sexuality. According to Freud, sexuality is composed of many different instincts which, if all goes well, integrate themselves into what may be understood as normal sexuality; if things do not go well, they appear as the so-called perversions.

We want to touch on Freud's theories only very briefly here. Freud describes in a very precise way the various stages which characterize human sexual development. For the newborn child, sexuality is still unorganized and diffuse. By nature the child is polymorphously-perversely autoerotic. The child contains, so to speak, all sexual tendencies which, if they are not integrated, we later experience as perversions.

The Nonsense of "Normal" Sexuality

The first centering of sexuality occurs in the area of the mouth. The first stage is the so-called oral phase, during which everything that has to do with the mouth—sucking, swallowing, eating—is experienced sexually. In the next phase these pleasurable feelings become more and more concentrated on the excretive organs and on the elimination of urine and feces. (To explain precisely why it is that sado-masochistic tendencies appear during this phase would go too far afield for our purposes.) In a still later phase, the genitalia take over the lead, and during this phallic stage (at about the age of five) enters the Oedipal phase with the incestuous desire for sexual contact with the father or mother. The Oedipal wishes are not fulfilled and must be repressed, and the result is the latency stage which lasts until about the twelfth year; during this phase the sexual instincts are repressed, and sexual energy is to some extent sublimated. During puberty the so-called normal sexuality finally comes into its own.

This long and complicated process of sexual development contains many dangers, through which sexual anomalies can come into being. In any phase a fixation can occur, and certain singular sexual components, as for instance anal sado-masochism or exhibitionism, can take over; or, out of anxiety about the strength of sexual instincts, displacement mechanisms can come into play through which the whole of sexuality gets concentrated on an avoidance object, as in the case of fetishism where the substitute-object plays the part of the thing desired.

According to Freud, the cause of this faulty development lies in a constitutional weakness or in congenital syphilis, in a weak nervous constitution, or in certain experiences which led to a fixation. Unfortunate sexual stimulation in a certain phase, as for example

the witnessing of sexual contact between the parents which is misunderstood as an attempt at murder, or seductions by relatives or
servants, can lead to the result that a certain part-instinct that is
important in the particular phase in question becomes all too important later and takes over.

In this regard such things as sexual deviancy were understood
as the dominance of overpowering infantile sexual instincts. Every
form of sexuality that did not in some way lead to classical sexual
intercourse had to be understood in this context as sexual perver-
sion.

This developmental schema of Freud's has been widely attacked in recent times. It has been shown, for example, that the
so-called latency period is a very questionable concept, in that
sexual life in children between the ages of six and twelve is in no
way diminished.

Unfortunately, the magnificence of Freud's thinking is often
not properly understood by the exponents of Jungian psychology.
Freud certainly does not describe "facts." His work can be best
appreciated if we understand his sexual theories as a modern mythology which, through its symbolic representations, gives us a better
entry into the world of sexuality than do statistical facts. Is not
perhaps the polymorphously perverse child, for instance, a symbolic representation of the whole person present in each child, in
whom everything is already to be found?

Freud attempted to demonstrate that several so-called perversions are present from the beginning in all people and that "normal" sexuality is nothing else than a delicate, artful creation whose
various building-blocks are the so-called perversions. It is the merit
of Freud's theory that sexual deviations are included in the under-

standing of sexuality and that the narrow understanding of sexuality is broadened beyond its connection to reproduction. The keen insights of Freud could not, however, break sexuality loose from its confinement once and for all. According to Gebsattel, for instance, masturbation is still a sin against the I-Thou principle, a sin against Eros, or, according to the famous Swiss psychologist and philosopher Paul Haeberlin, a sin against the partner.

The existentialists attempted in part to understand the richness of sexuality more deeply. Medard Boss holds that not only normal sexuality but every variety of sexuality is a desperate, if sometimes limited, attempt to express love. Other existentialists understand sexual instinct as a drive to be in the world, and they consider that when there occurs a split between the world and the instinct, this split must be filled in with sexual fantasies and sexual perversions of a destructive nature, like sadism and masochism.

For our own further inquiry, however, we want to remember Freud's statement, that "perhaps nowhere else does all-powerful love show itself more strongly than in the aberrations."

Any approach to sexuality which would have reproduction— or even the formal sexual act— as *the* central focus, and which would see all other sexual activity as suspect, must be judged in the light of the following phenomena:

In psychotherapeutic practice it happens again and again that the more differentiated, and *not* the weaker, the person is, the more we find the so-called sexual aberrations. Exceptions prove the rule. Undifferentiated people, with minimal affective development and cultural stimulation, possess a "normal" sexuality far more frequently than do affectively and culturally differentiated people.

Sexuality and Individuation

Furthermore, hardly anyone who has made the attempt to understand sexuality has taken note of the fact that the greatest portion of human sexual life consists of fantasies; in part, these are of the "normal" variety, but in part they are also of a very remarkable variety—significantly more remarkable than the actually-lived sexual life.

We need to find a key to sexual life, and to the sexual aberrations that belong to it, which will make it possible for us to understand everything, the whole sexual phenomenon in all its variety and richness, without moralizing or biologizing it, without dogmatizing about what should or should not be.

SEXUALITY AND INDIVIDUATION

I would like to try to enlarge the reader's understanding of sexuality. Without such a broad understanding, the role of sexuality and of its variations in marriage cannot be fully comprehended. Unfortunately, many of the most modern and up-to-date methods of studying sexuality do not get us very far. The attempt, for example, to assert that sexuality is nothing but a pleasurable experience does not seem to me to comprehend all of the phenomena. The compelling power of sexuality, the fact that most people devote a great part of their fantasy to sexual themes, the enormous problem that sexuality has been in every age—all of this is not accidental and would be completely unintelligible were it true that it had to do only with the experience of a simple pleasure. Sexuality has always had something of the numinous about it, something uncanny and fascinating. The fact, for instance, that there was temple prostitution in historical times in the Orient does not mean that these peoples perceived sexuality as something "natural," as something that one could experience in a frivolous and pleasurable way. It indicates just the opposite: these peoples experienced sexuality as something so numinous that it could even take place in a temple.

Sexuality understood as a form of interpersonal relationship between man and woman also does not fully embrace the phenomenon of sexuality. Most sexual fantasies are played out quite independently of human relationships. They have to do with people with whom one would hardly have any relationship at all, or with whom a relationship would even be impossible.

Neither the understanding of sexuality as interpersonal relationship nor as a pleasure on the same level as eating and drinking advances us very far in the understanding of this human phenomenon. Neither procreation, nor pleasure, nor interpersonal relationship explains the enormous variety of sexual life and sexual fantasy.

Freud sought in his own very impressive way to understand all of the so-called higher activities of man (such as art, religion, etc.) as sublimated sexuality. We can attempt to turn this around and to ask: can the totality of sexuality be comprehended from the viewpoint of individuation, of the religious impulse? Are the deeply sexually-colored love songs of medieval nuns really, as Freud would have it, expressions of frustrated eroticism? Do the many modern songs and the old folk-songs that sing sentimentally about love and leave-taking have to do only with the unlived sexuality of adolescence? Or are they symbolic forms of expression for individuation processes and for the religious quest?

Sexuality and Individuation

It is worthwhile to try to bring sexuality into relation with individuation. One of the tasks of individuation, as already mentioned, is to become acquainted with the personal, collective, and archetypal shadow. This means not only pushing through to the apparently destructive layers of the soul by virtue of personal or collective circumstances; it also entails making contact with "evil" itself, with the murderer and the suicidal killer within us. Another no less important task of the individuation process is for men to confront the feminine, and women the masculine, sides of themselves, to have a confrontation with the anima and animus. The struggle with the contrasexual side and the awareness of one's mysterious bond to it provide the opportunity to experience and to understand the polarities of the soul and of the world, of man and woman, human being and God, good and evil, conscious and unconscious, rational and irrational. The so-called *coniunctio oppositorum*, the union or convergence of the opposites, is one of the many models and symbols for the goal of individuation.

Jung repeatedly emphasized the importance of dreams, fantasies, active imagination, religious mythology, and artistic work in the individuation process. Through these media we can experience the symbols through which we individuate. Here we see the living symbols which transform us. Symbols have the tendency to become the possession of a small educated elite. This happened, for example, to the Greek Gods in the course of history. The same thing could happen with the Christian symbols. The Gods of ancient Greece are perhaps symbols of spiritual powers, of archetypes, but the Greeks themselves experienced them sensually, as concrete realities. As the peoples of the antique world began to take their Gods symbolically, to understand the Gods consciously as symbols, the Gods lost much of their influence on the spiritual life of most of the people. We psychologists, too, for all of our more or less deep understanding of symbols, have a great desire for concreteness. Analysts always fall into the attempt, for instance, of interpreting dreams not as symbol but as concrete oracle; thus the mother's appearance in a dream is all too often taken as the physical mother, rather than as the symbol of the maternal.

The Greeks honored their Gods and sacrificed to them; they could experience them most intensely, particularly their archetypal components, in their own souls—through projection, as we say today. The process of individuation in general is often experienced in projection. The medieval alchemists projected their spiritual development into the actual or fantasied chemical processes. But the Greeks' concrete experience of the Olympian Gods, the alchemists' of material, was a limited individuation process. C.G. Jung emphasized many times the importance of "taking back" projections. When projections are taken back, then dreams, fantasies, and active imagination become the actual medium of the individuation process, thus making it possible to encounter living symbols that can actually work on us.

Individuation needs living symbols. But where today do we find living, working, symbols? Symbols that are as living and effective as the Gods of the ancient Greeks or as the alchemical process? At just this point a new understanding of sexuality reveals itself to us. Sexuality is not identical with reproduction, and its meaning is not exhausted in human relationships or in the experience of pleasure. Sexuality, with all its variations, can be understood as an individuation fantasy, a fantasy whose symbols are so alive and so effective that they even influence our physiology. And as an aside, the symbols are not the exclusive possession of an academic elite, but the possession of all people.

What are the possibilities, then, for a man to come to terms with the feminine? One possibility obtains in a relationship to a woman, as in marriage for example; another can consist in sexual fantasies, including homosexual—where the feminine can be experienced with another man—whose goal is not reproduction, human relationship, or pleasure, but the confrontation with the anima, with the feminine.

The sexual fantasies of most men and women are wilder and more bizarre than actual sexual life as it is lived. Unfortunately, analysts and psychologists often react to such fantasies condescendingly and pathologize them. A commentary on a particularly lively and unusual sexual fantasy of a patient might be the following: "This young man—or woman—is not yet capable of relationship. He is still completely the victim of his non-human sexual instinct." Or an analyst says to a colleague during a case discussion: "He misuses his girlfriend in order to live out his sexual fantasies. He still lacks tenderness and sensitivity." Another commentary: "This old man is suffering from senile lecherousness." The expression, "he escapes into fantasy," is often heard as well. This kind of condescending, pathologizing way of looking at these phenomena works destructively on the soul. Individuation takes place not only in projection and human relationship. The process must take place inwardly, through the means of symbols: not merely through reflection and thought, but through symbols which seize soul *and* body, and thereby seize the whole man in their grasp.

I would like to emphasize once more that sexual life, above

all as it shows itself in fantasy, is an intense individuation process in symbols. This form of the process must be respected and recognized. It is unpsychological to understand this phenomenon as something primitive, which may have a certain symbolic meaning but which should be sublimated and thereby experienced on a higher plane. It is damaging to the soul when sexual life becomes too spiritualized. However, here I must prevent misunderstanding: my recommendation has nothing necessarily to do with an intensive living-out of sexuality, as advocated by Wilhelm Reich, for example. Sexual life and particularly fantasies about it with their many peculiar and beautiful features represent only one of many media wherein individuation takes place; it is not *the* medium *par excellence.*

I would like to demonstrate with the following example that even the most remarkable sexual fantasies and practices have a connection with individuation, and hence with salvation.

I once treated a student, a fetishist, who had gotten into conflict with the police because of stealing female underwear. I was myself still in psychiatric training at that time, and I tried to help this student by uncovering certain psychodynamic connections. One day he came in and with a triumphant voice read to me the passage where Faust meets Helen. He read to me how Faust, after a long search, finally stood facing the most beautiful feminine creature in the whole world, the beautiful Helen, and how she disappeared leaving Faust standing there with her garment and veil in his hands.

"Women are only a symbol anyway," he explained to me. "Maybe the experience of meeting the feminine is deeper if one has only a piece of her clothing, an object which symbolizes the woman, rather than having the woman herself. At least one then never forgets that the fantasy is almost as important as the reality."

In a certain sense this student was right. He did not equate sexuality with reproduction, with pure pleasure, or with human relationship. He understood it as something symbolic. Through him it became clear to me that sexuality had to be understood differently from the way I had understood it until then. I began to wonder if it is not often the case that sexual deviation comes closer to the phenomenon of sexuality than does so-called normal sexuality. I must repeat: the concepts "normal" and "abnormal" have lost some of their meaning with respect to sexual life. Individuation provides us with the key to *sexuality,* and not to normality or abnormality.

As I mentioned earlier, one of the great tasks of the individuation process is to experience the dark, destructive side. This can occur through the medium of sexuality, which can be one of many possible places for this experience. This certainly does not mean that one must be inundated by the fantasies of a Marquis de Sade or of a Leopold Sacher-Masoch, or that one should enact such fantasies. It means rather that fantasies of such a kind can be understood as the symbolical expression of an individuation process which is unfolding in the territory of the sexual Gods.

I once treated a masochistic woman, a self-flagellator, whom I tried to help to normalize herself. I even had some success: her masochistic activities stopped, and she suppressed her masochistic fantasies. However she began to suffer from an inexplicable headache that caused her great problems in her professional life. In a sort of visionary experience—she was a black African woman and in her environment such things were not uncommon—Moses appeared to her and instructed her to continue with her flagellations; if she did not do so, the Egyptians would kill her. On the basis of this vision she developed a complicated theory, based in part on the flagellation rituals of the Mexican Christians, which held that only through her masochism could she confront and come to terms with the suffering of the world. She allowed herself once more to be overcome by masochistic fantasies; as she did so, her headaches disappeared and her psychological development proceeded very well. This example is meant to serve as an illustration, not as a recommendation.

The phenomenon of sado-masochism has often stimulated the wonder of psychologists. How can pleasure and pain coincide? Masochism seems to be something self-contradictory for many psychologists and psychoanalysts. Some of them go so far as to maintain that masochists may try now and then to act out their fantasies in great detail and with much theatricality, but when it actually comes down to suffering they immediately cease such behavior. However, this is not altogether correct, and moreover it relates in part to certain sexual variations. Actual sexual life is seldom fully in accord with sexual fantasies. We know that there exist many masochists who not only seek out degrading forms of pain but also experience them with pleasure.

Masochism played a large role in the Middle Ages, when flagellators flooded through the cities and villages. Many of the saints devoted much time to beating themselves. Monks and nuns considered it routine practice to inflict pain and humiliation upon themselves. The attempt of modern psychiatry to understand this whole collective phenomenon as an expression of perverse and neurotic sexuality does not seem satisfying to me. We come closer to the phenomenon with the concept of individuation. Is not the suffering of our life, and of life in general, one of the most difficult things there is to accept? The world is so full of suffering, and all of us suffer so greatly in body and spirit, that even the saints have difficulty understanding this. It is one of the most difficult tasks of the individuation process to accept sorrow and joy, pain and pleasure, God's anger and God's grace. The opposites—suffering and joy, pain and pleasure—are symbolically united in masochism. Thus life can be actually accepted, and even pain can be joyfully experienced. The masochist, in a remarkable and fantastic way, confronts and comes to terms with the greatest opposites of our existence.

Rape plays a large role in the dreams and fantasies of women. It is often even the center of compulsive fears. Whether frightening, exciting, or alluring, the fantasy of rape is in each case often important for the feminine psyche. Rape is one of the great themes of Greek mythology and of the plastic arts. Perhaps the rape motif has something to do with the soul's being suddenly and brutally overwhelmed by the spirit: the animus overruns the willing-unwilling feminine soul. In my psychotherapeutic practice I have often seen how the fantasy of rape, understood as a psychological value, as a living symbol, as something which need not and cannot be either reduced or conquered, has kept the patient moving, and helped her on the way to individuation.

Perhaps it is gradually becoming understandable why we want to free ourselves from the "dominant images of normality." It is this holding-on to a so-called normal sexuality that makes a true understanding of sexuality impossible. A large portion of the sexual fantasies of mankind, when looked at from the viewpoint of conceptions of normality, are very peculiar. We cannot understand a psychological phenomenon if we explain a considerable portion of it simply as abnormal or pathological.

I would like to demonstrate here that the so-called perversions are essential to an understanding of sexuality. So as not to evade the difficulties, I have approached one of the seemingly least intelligible variations of sexual life, masochism. What we have begun we want now to follow out to a conclusion. Masochism is almost always combined with sadism. One speaks of sado-masochism. For the psychologist committed to the biological view, who believes he can explain all of psychological life on the basis of survival mechanisms, masochism is a stumbling block. Remarkably enough, sadism seems to pose fewer intellectual difficulties; access to this phenomenon has been obstructed primarily due to moral preconceptions.

First, then, a few conceptual clarifications. In the instance of classical sadism, we understand sexual pleasure achieved through causing or observing physical or psychological pain in the partner. By sadism in the broader sense we understand simply cruelty, namely, the enjoyment derived from hurting someone else physically or psychologically, without necessarily gaining from this a sense of sexual pleasure. By moral sadism is understood the tendency to find joy in making other people suffer psychologically. Aggression, in contrast, is something that has little to do with the phenomenon just mentioned, but it is often mixed up with it. Aggression is the ability and the joy of having one's way, of conquering the enemy, or overcoming, of mastering a situation through activity, of coming in "first" in a contest with one's fellows. Aggression in this sense is an important survival instinct. Bringing pain to others is not essential to aggression; its essence is rather to prove oneself forcefully. Because sadism is often mistakenly confused with aggression, which can easily be understood from the biological point of view, it seems to present fewer intellectual difficulties than does masochism.

The joy of seeing other people suffer physically or psychologically is very common, much more frequent than pure sexual sadism. Nonetheless a muted sexual tone often accompanies the kind of cruelty that is not in itself particularly sexually-colored.

Cruelty, the joy of torturing one's fellow man, has been described since the beginnings of man's recorded behavior; it occupies our fantasies and fills our movies. The Romans, for example, whose civilization and culture stand as a fundamental pillar of the Western world, knew little inhibition in this regard. For their amusement they threw slaves and criminals to wild animals. When a crucifixion was to take place in a theatrical piece, they actually crucified a criminal on stage.

Peter the Great of Russia is supposed to have presented beheadings for the amusement of his guests. Mary, Queen of Scots, in her youth as Dauphine de France, had to watch Huguenots being tortured to death during her dessert. Public executions were in all periods great folk-festivals. On such occasions grandmothers lifted their small grandchildren up on their shoulders so that they would be sure to see everything. And the cruelties of World War II are familiar to us all.

Cruelty for the sake of sexual pleasure, too, has been described since the beginning of historical time. The Marquis de Sade, a French nobleman of the eighteenth century, is in our time the best-known author to deal with this phenomenon.

The greatest portion of sadistic sexuality, however, occurs in the fantasies and dreams of people. In sadism, psychological components show themselves which are of the greatest importance for a person's development.

Sadism is in part to be understood as an expression of the destructive side of people: an expression of the core, of the shadow, of the murderer within us. It is a specifically human trait to find joy in destruction. This is not the place to consider whether destructiveness belongs to human nature or is the product of a faulty development, although I believe the former to be true. In any case, destructiveness is a psychological phenomenon with which every living human being must come to terms. The joy of destroying, of obliterating, of torturing, etc., is also experienced within the sexual medium.

The joy of destroying others is related to self-destructiveness. Thus it is not surprising that sadism and masochism appear together: the self-destructive killer is the center of the archetypal shadow, the center of irreducible destructiveness in human beings.

Another component in sadism is the intoxication with power. It provides sexual pleasure to dominate the partner completely, to play with him like a cat with a mouse.

Still another aspect of sadism is to degrade the partner to the status of pure object. In sadistic fantasies, the binding of the partner and the "cool" watching of his reactions plays a great role. The partner becomes purely a thing whose reactions are played with.

This sadistic objectification plays quite a large role in many sexual relationships. Any human relationship, sexual or otherwise, should always be an encounter of two equally entitled partners — so it is claimed. And as soon as the other becomes an object, be it in order to gain pleasure or to observe him with interest, the relationship is unhealthy.

I believe, however, we are being led too much by prejudices

here. Every relationship is in part composed of an objectification. It is also necessary to be able to observe the partner impartially and completely objectively. On the one hand, we experience in love a full identification with the other; on the other hand, a cool objectivity should not be avoided. Without objectivity a relationship remains chaotic and dangerous. How often we hear it said during divorce actions: "I loved him so much and now this has happened; I simply don't know him anymore. He has changed so; he is another person." This disappointment, this surprise, occurs mostly in relationships in which objectivity was neglected.

In sadism then, destruction, power, and objectification express themselves in the sexual medium.

I am only attempting to point out the individuational character of sexuality, not to glorify the perversions. In this connection it seems correct to show that the broad range of human sexual activity, particularly as it manifests in sexual fantasies, need not be understood *only* as pathology.

The individuational aspect of sexuality reveals itself most compellingly in the loving, intense encounter between man and woman, in the momentary, ecstatic fusing together of the love act. This most deeply moving of human experiences cannot be grasped as merely biological copulation. This powerful event in which man and woman become one, physically and psychologically, is to be understood as a living symbol of the *mysterium coniunctionis*, the goal of the way of individuation. The sexual union of the King and Queen was considered by the alchemists to be the crowning of their work. Sexual fusion expresses the bridging in us of all the prevailing oppositions and incompatibilities. To an extent man and woman complete one another, to an extent they are not at all synchronized with one another. In the love act the whole polarity and fragmentation of being is overcome. This is its fascination, not the associated possibility of a reproductive result. The act of love is moreover much more than merely an expression of the personal relationship between a certain man and a certain woman. It is a symbol for something that goes beyond the personal relationship. This explains the frequent appearance of erotic images in the description of religious experiences. The mystical union with God is in part symbolized by the love act. In this sense most of the love stories of the world, the love poems and the songs about the union of man and woman, are not to be understood as merely the expression of erotic life, but as religious symbols. Freud demonstrates most impressively how all of the sexual part-instincts find their way together in the sexual act to form a great experience. Coming out of the remarkable and fascinating variety of sexual drives, the sexual act occurs as a great event.

Sexual life and erotic fantasies are so rich and multifaceted that every possible variety of psychological life can be experienced through this living symbolism. As Jung understood the peculiar activities and images of the alchemists to be images of psychological development and individuation, so we can recognize and follow the process of individuation in sexual life and its variations. In this connection we also understand the greatness of Freud. He believed he could describe sexuality within the biological model, but he described it with unusual differentiation, and he thought that he had discovered in it the foundations of human behavior. Only a psychologist of the Jungian school can grasp Freudian psychology; Freud encountered sexuality and was overwhelmed by its fascinating manifestations. Against his own intentions, so to speak, he created a modern, living sexual mythology. As an example of this, consider again the image of the polymorphously perverse child: it exists in each of us throughout our whole lives. Some aspects of it are repressed, and lead a merely shadow existence in dreams and mysterious fantasies. What is this polymorphously perverse child if not the Self of Jungian psychology, the symbol of the totality of the psyche, the divine core within us which contains everything, all the possibilities and opposites of our psyche?

I want to mention here one further characteristic of sexual life with all of its variations which can only really be understood from the viewpoint of the individuation process. I am thinking of shyness and secrecy. Sexual life, whether lived-out or fantasied, is kept secret by most people. Even in the analytical situation it can take years before the deepest sexual fantasies are surrendered. Most of the sexual images which appear in the dreams of patients are rendered harmless and cleaned up. This desire for secrecy is hardly comprehensible from the viewpoint of reproduction, pleasure, or human relationship. Mystery and intimacy are, however, characteristics of the soul and of the individuation process. For a time this process must proceed in a closed vessel; nothing and no one dare disturb it.

THE DEMONIC SIDE OF SEXUALITY

I have indicated above that for a long time Christian theologians could recognize sexuality only in connection with reproduction. They experienced the erotic as something demonic and uncanny, as something that had to be fought against or neutralized. All of these medieval theologians were certainly intelligent and differentiated people, in honest search for truth and understanding. That they experienced sexuality as demonic, therefore, cannot be so easily discounted. They were expressing something quite true.

Sexuality is still demonized in our day. All attempts to render it completely harmless and to present it as something completely "natural" flounder and fail. To modern man, sexuality in certain forms continues to appear as something evil and sinfully sinister.

Certain women's liberation movements try to understand sexuality as a political weapon used by men to suppress women; thus they demonize sexuality, while at the same time implying that by an exchange of roles between man and woman sexuality can become harmless.

As another example of demonization I would like to cite the purported effect of the so-called primal scene. Students of Freud, and a large portion of educated official opinion under their influence, hold that one must expect serious psychological consequences in a child who has accidentally witnessed sexual contact between its parents. Many neurotic developments are attributed to such childhood experiences.

94

The Demonic Side of Sexuality

Something about this theory seems peculiar: ninety percent of humanity lives in housing conditions which make it impossible that children will not accidentally witness the sexual activities of their parents. Only a very small part of humanity is economically able to house a family in more than one or two rooms. The observation of sexual contact between parents or other adults certainly does impress children very deeply. Whether such an experience, however, which belongs to the childhood of most people, actually moves someone towards neurosis has still to be proven. This would mean that experiences which belong unavoidably to the childhood of most people create serious damage. This is extremely unlikely, unless one understands sexuality as something in itself sinister, possessing an almost magical power.

To avoid any misunderstanding: it seems to me that modern psychologists who carry the removal of taboos so far as to recommend to parents *not* to exclude children from their sexual life are throwing out the baby with the bathwater. The authors of modern children's books who believe that the sexual life of parents should be shown in their books are, in my opinion, very naive. They overlook the incest complex, which expresses itself in the universally-acknowledged incest taboo. An unrestricted presentation of the sexual activities of parents overstimulates the incestuous wishes and related jealousy of children. Through this, the Oedipal situation gets uncomfortably intensified. On the other hand, it is fortunately impossible for very many parents to show their sexuality to their children openly and without inhibition. This too is related to the incest taboo. The parents as well defend themselves instinctively against overstimulation of their incest fantasies and tendencies. The repression of a taboo probably creates

95

more psychological damage than does the respectful recognition of it. Some of the greatest taboos, like the incest taboo, protect us more than they restrict us.

This is not the place to take up an exhaustive discussion of the incest taboo. Nevertheless, we might take note of the fact that the incest taboo probably cannot be understood as biologically motivated. Had people practiced incest, they would have increased unfavorable hereditary factors among themselves. Children with such unfavorable hereditary factors would, for the most part, have died off, and thus mankind as a whole would have had far fewer unfavorable hereditary factors in its gene pool. The incest taboo is not, therefore, to be explained as instinctive eugenics. Surely the incest taboo is connected with the human impulse to develop ever further, and to always be in a position of confronting new souls. Close heterosexual bonds must always be forged outside of the immediate family so that human development will not stagnate.

Another example of the widespread opinion that sexuality is something magically damaging is expressed in the laws and in the juridical attitude regarding exhibitionism. Experiences with exhibitionists are undoubtedly frightening to many children and to adult women. But that this scare damages the soul of the victim to such an extent that exhibitionists should be frightened off by long prison sentences or even by forcible castration is questionable. It is impossible to demonstrate conclusively that any child has ever been severely damaged by such an experience, let alone that a grown woman has suffered serious psychological damage from it.

We know that exhibitionists are as a rule harmless, and they expose themselves because they are afraid of the female sex and do not trust themselves to get close to women. The danger of being raped by a so-called normal man is much greater than the danger of being mistreated in this way by an exhibitionist.

It is true that many adults who suffer from sexual problems claim that these originate from a certain childhood experience of theirs, for instance from an encounter with an exhibitionist, but such attempts at explanation are not to be taken as proof of such an etiology. The desire in people to find a causal explanation is very strong. When a person suffers from an upset stomach he will blame the cold beer that he drank the day before; many homosexuals, when they experience social pain for their homosexuality or are indicted for it, will try to trace their homosexuality back to an encounter with an exhibitionist.

Another contemporary example of how sexuality is still experienced as sinister is found in the regimentation and exclusion of sexuality from most of our hospitals. When it is a case of the patient's spending only a short time in the hospital, this is not a great problem. But that every form of sexual life is banned for patients who have to spend an extended period of time in a hospital, as in mental institutions, sanatoriums for tuberculosis, etc., can be explained only by the demonization of sexuality. It is believed that a sexual life could in some puzzling, mysterious way harm these needy patients. But why is this believed? For what reason are the patients in a mental institution, for instance, not allowed to have sexual contact with one another within the institution?

The following is yet another example of how it is taken for granted that sexuality must be something sinister. Sexual inter-

course with a mentally retarded person is considered a criminal act
in Switzerland. The intent of this law was to protect the mentally
retarded person from being misused. But the basic effect of this
law was to make it impossible for the mentally retarded to have
a sexual life. That such an inhumane law has not run into popular
resistance demonstrates once again that an almost magical power
is attributed to sexuality.

One last example. Athletes—the participants in the Olympics for instance—are often strictly forbidden by their coaches
to engage in any sexual activities during the contests. It has happened that athletes in the Olympics have been sent home for en-
gaging in surreptitious sexual adventures. Yet, at the same time,
it is known to be beneficial for certain athletes to be sexually active before undertaking great athletic efforts.

Ancient prejudices are at work here. Among certain primi-
tives the men dare not have sexual contact with women before
going into battle.

The demonic element within sexuality shows itself also perhaps in the fact that it is very difficult to experience and to accept sexual activities purely as "enjoyment" or pleasurable experience. Few people can "simply enjoy" sexuality as they would a
good meal. The "glass of water theory"—sexual experience as the
quenching of thirst—is frequently advocated but seldom experienced by people over a long period of time.

What does it mean for psychology that sexuality always has
something sinister about it, even today when we believe that we
have liberated ourselves from this attitude? The sinister is always
the unintelligible, the impressive, the numinous. Wherever something divine appears, we begin to experience fear. The individua-

tion process, which has a strongly religious character, is experienced as numinous in many respects. Everything that has to do with salvation possesses, among other things, a sinister, unfamiliar character; it always includes the superhuman.

The demonization of sexuality is perhaps understandable given its individuational character. It is not simply a harmless biological activity, but rather a symbol for something that relates to the meaning of our lives, to our striving and longing for the divine.

Sexuality offers us symbols for all aspects of individuation. The encounter with the parental figures is experienced in the incest drama. The confrontation with the shadow leads to the destructive sado-masochistic components of the erotic. The encounter with one's own soul, with the anima and animus, with the feminine and the masculine, can have a sexual form. Self-love and love for others is experienced bodily in sexuality, whether via fantasies or activities. Nowhere is the union of all the opposites, the *unio mystica*, the *mysterium coniunctionis*, more impressively expressed than in the language of eroticism.

FULL SEXUALITY IN MARRIAGE

I have emphasized that individuation can take place by various ways and means; there is not only one road to Rome. Salvation can be obtained in a thousand different ways. Not only one form of individuation is open to a person, but rather many at the same time, all of which distinguish themselves from the others.

Individuation through sexuality, i.e., through sexual symbols, I would like to describe as *instinctual individuation.* It is pressed upon us, given, without our having to make great decisions about it. For this reason, sexual individuation-symbolism is so important: in it appear the most colors, images, and stories for every manner of individuation.

A fundamentally different form of individuation is what I described above as the "confrontation marriage." One chooses to get married; one makes a choice in this. Individuation through marriage I would like to classify as one of the *decision-individuations.* One decides to enter a marriage in the same way as one decides to go into analysis, to take up a certain profession, etc.

Marriage and sexuality have been closely bound up with one another since time immemorial. Women have been, and still are, forbidden in many cultures to experience sexuality outside of marriage. Young girls had to be virginal when they married. The laws today are still firm on this point: sexual relations outside of marriage are looked upon as adultery. In a marriage that is above all understood as a way to salvation, sexuality is naturally an ideal field for the quest after the salvation of individuation. In such a marriage sexuality does not serve the purpose of reproduction, nor merely the interpersonal relationship and the mutuality of love; rather it serves the passion for individuation.

For this reason there is no such thing as normal (or perverse) sexuality among married people. Everything is possible, everything is allowed, since everything is the expression of individuation fantasies. And yet there are always married couples whose sexuality is constricted by a certain pressure for normality. Each partner allows himself to be revealed to the other only within certain boundaries, and each refrains from what is believed to be

100

really not permissible. Therefore it turns out that a husband and wife only rarely fulfill one another completely. Instead of each of them encouraging the other to express and relate his most secret and most peculiar sexual fantasies, a certain fear of abnormality dominates the scene, even a tendency toward a moralistic condemnation of anything that does not unconditionally belong to one of the partners. The result of this is that individuation material is excluded from the marriage or lived out elsewhere or, what is almost equally serious, the one partner passively—though reproachfully—goes along.

In marriage it is advisable to live out the shared sexual interests and if possible to accept those that are different, or in any case not reject them. In this way one learns to know the other person in all of his heights and depths. Thus one actively traverses the soul's primeval forest, and as we saw in the myth of Culhwrch, not every deed has to be performed by oneself.

In certain marriages, however, this can be very difficult. The man, for example, has bisexual interests. How should his wife react to this? Should she encourage him to tell his homosexual fantasies in which she has no interest, or even encourage him to live out his homosexuality? General rules for this cannot be given; only the attitude with which to approach such problems can be discussed. It is desirable for everyone in such ambiguous circumstances to go further in his tolerance than his own inclinations would otherwise lead him. One rule would be that for the sake of staying together until death, one try not to evade the other sexually, just as one would not evade the other psychologically. The confrontation never ends. Just how this is lived out is the business of each individual married couple and of each partner. Each couple creates

101

its salvation within the marriage and seeks there its unique individuation. In this sense, married persons are completely sovereign and bound to no conceptions of normality. Every single marriage is a world unto itself. "All's fair in love and war."

The independence of every single marriage from every sort of standard and criterion relates not only to sexual behavior but to the total being of the individual marriage partners.

To this I must add something of more general significance. The so-called normal, completely unneurotic person is hardly to be found. Each of us tries, in his own peculiar way, with more or less success, to wrestle with the fundamental, insoluble problems and contradictions of life, such as: the longing to be taken care of, to enjoy childish dependency on the one hand and independent existence on the other, to be free from parents and to remain a child forever; the desire for other people and the fear of them and of one's own aggression; the anxiety about pain and physical decay; the fear of death and the aspiration to live forever through children and grandchildren; the wish for power and the wish for subordination; love and hate; piety and hubris, etc. In this regard everyone is more or less neurotic. Our psychological abilities to come to terms with the powers of the soul are various and diverse.

It never happens, therefore, that in marriage two completely "healthy" people get together. Both have their neurotic peculiarities and distortions. But marriage does not have to do with one partner's curing the other, or even with one's changing the other significantly; this is not possible. Through the act of getting married, one has taken on the task of mutual confrontation until death. The marriage has to work somehow, i.e., the neurotic symptoms too will have to be synchronized with one another.

The peculiarities of oneself and of one's partner must be borne, accepted, and integrated into the interplay between the spouses. It is very impressive how much extremely pathological behavior an individuation marriage is able to bear. In almost every good marriage the accomplished psychologist can find a sufficient number of neurotic mechanisms to consider the marriage impossible and ripe for divorce. In the individuation marriage, both partners confront each other with everything, with the healthy and the sick, the normal and the abnormal traits of their essential being.

Many marriages dry up and miss the path to individuation because the couples try to ease their situations through excluding and repressing their most important essential characteristics, whether these be peculiar sexual wishes, neurotic traits, or whatever. The more one confronts everything, the more interesting and fruitful becomes the path to individuation.

MARRIAGE IS NOT A PRIVATE MATTER

One of the most frequent ways in which a marriage partner "brackets out" part of his psyche today is by isolating himself from his larger family, from his parents, etc.

The intrusion of in-laws into marriages always leads to considerable difficulties. In countless popular jokes and cartoons it is shown, for instance, how the mother-in-law pops up in the doorway to the fearful surprise of the son-in-law. Disturbing influences of relatives have brought many marriages to the edge of divorce. Certain relatives are always a problem. The mother interferes too much;

the father does not understand the son-in-law; the wife admires her father more than her husband; one is ashamed of parents because they come from a different social milieu, or are greedy about money, or have no spirit; a certain nephew tells dirty jokes all the time, etc.

Many marriage counselors and analysts recommend in such cases pulling away from the relationship with the family, or even breaking it off. Perhaps in some cases this may be absolutely correct, but from the standpoint of marriage as a way of individuation it is usually very questionable. If we take seriously the idea of the collective unconscious as C.G. Jung understood it, we are not only vaguely bound up with the psyche of all people but especially so with the souls of both the nearest and the most distant family relatives. To express it somewhat more concretely, the souls of our nearest and most distant relatives are to be found in our unconscious. They are a part of us and we of them.

To break off contact with the immediate and more extended family means nothing less than repressing something. The family members are always still in our soul, but they are no longer concretized through sitting at our table.

Confrontation in marriage serves individuation the best when it is as inclusive as possible, when it includes so far as possible all the parts of our soul. A confrontational dialectical encounter with the family of the partner belongs therefore to a particular psychological process; it belongs to the special way of salvation.

An individuation marriage is seldom a private matter. This is expressed in most marriage ceremonies, wherein the near and distant relatives take part and belong to the ceremony. The contemporary custom of conducting a marriage in the smallest possible

104

circle does not express the reality of marriage with an adequate ritual. Such ceremonies are signs of a psychologically unrealistic individualism. Each person is seen as an isolated individual unrelated to the collective unconscious which binds him to all other people — most of all to his own family.

I have discovered that married persons who separate themselves from their families often function relatively well but become exceedingly sterile and boring.

Here is an example. The wife came from a so-called "primitive" family. Her father was a successful tradesman who struck one as psychologically undifferentiated and crude. Her mother seemed to fade into the household and had no cultural or spiritual interests. The conversation of the parents and siblings of the wife revolved around television programs and the latest news in the popular daily.

The husband came from a middle-class, somewhat boring family whose members tended towards depression. His mother took her life when he was about twenty years old. A brother of his saw everything as negative, and could choke every joy with his pessimism.

After their marriage, which they celebrated with only a small circle of friends, the couple more or less broke off relations with their families. He was bored and disgusted with his depressive relatives, and she was ashamed of her family.

The marriage proceeded on the whole rather peacefully but impressed the married pair themselves as rather boring, and it struck the few friends of the young family as exceedingly sterile and uninteresting.

Then the wife had the following dream: She is arguing in a

crude manner with her father. As some people approach, she begins to be ashamed and is afraid that these people will get excited about the crude language of the conflict. She pushes her father away from her, and he falls into some water. It is unclear whether she intentionally pushed him into the water, but in any case he sinks without a sound. Then someone from the crowd says to the dreamer: "He (i.e., the father) knows how to invest money at the highest interest..."

It would lead too far afield to take up all the associations of the dreamer. Here is just one of them: to "interest" she associated the unused, buried talent in the New Testament. The analysand was interested in everything financial and also understood something about it.

Together with the association, the dream wanted to say something like this: because she pushed the father away into the water, into sinking out of sight, no one was there anymore who knew how to invest money at interest. What this means is that the woman had become unfruitful and could no longer give a good return on her talents.

THE SACRIFICE

The marriage of St. Joseph, as we understand it, is one in which both marriage partners renounce sexuality; it is thus an a-sexual marriage. Today this marriage is gently ridiculed as a peculiar "Catholic institution." Psychiatrists and psychologists would describe such a marriage, in the event that the cause of the asexuality were not an organic illness, as the neurotic arrangement of two people who were severely disturbed in their psychological development. In our day, the psycho-hygienists demand of everyone, from their youth to their old age, a healthy and vigorous sexual life. No healthy married person, and no healthy single person, is supposed to lead an asexual life. Healthy, vigorous sexuality is *de rigueur.*

This is a conformist, leveling demand. It confuses people with animals; it requires that a person live "naturally," and sexuality is counted as part of this naturalism.

There are lots of people who have no great interest in sexuality and are not severely "neurotic." Occasionally one finds a married couple for whom sexuality is only mildly interesting. Such a marriage is positively *not* absurd. Within marriage it is possible, as in practically no other situation, for sexuality-as-individuational-symbol to be lived out completely. But the goal of marriage is not sexual experience, but rather salvation, individuation: to seek and to find God, the soul, and oneself. And this can also happen without sexuality.

This leads us to a central problem of marriage, of salvation, and individuation. We Jungian psychologists often speak of becoming whole, of fulfilling oneself completely, rather than speaking of individuation. The "whole person" is the goal of the long road to individuation. The mandala, a symbol for the goal or center of individuation, has the form of a circle and symbolically contains all the opposites; in it nothing is lacking.

But such a process of becoming complete is not necessarily implied in the word "salvation," and the phrase "to become whole" or "complete" is open to misunderstanding. Individuation, as the quest for salvation, has to do not only with becoming whole; it also demands renunciatory sacrifice. Something must be given away or given up, or to put it paradoxically: to the process of achieving wholeness belongs the sacrifice, the actual renunciation, of living parts of our personality, of that which may be most valuable in and to us.

Mythologically and ritually, the sacrifice always plays a large role. On the one hand, it is extolled; on the other, it remains a stumbling block and a cause of vexation. Here the remarkable story of Abraham and Isaac comes to mind. God demands of Abraham that he sacrifice his son Isaac. At the last moment, however, God prevents the sacrifice. We should not be led astray by the conclusion to this story. Even mythological stories have a tendency to comfort (though to a lesser degree than fairy tales) so as not to frighten the listener unduly. Whether or not God actually received the sacrifice of Abraham is inconsequential. He demanded it, and that means he could have accepted it. He requires that Abraham be prepared to offer the sacrifice of his son. This is not so much the story of a testing, of an attempt on the part of God to find out if Abraham would be ready to sacrifice his son; the central issue of the story is that God *requires* this sacrifice.

I recall also a story about Agamemnon and Iphigenia. The Greeks can sail for Asia Minor and conquer the city of Troy only after Agamemnon has sacrificed his daughter. This mythological tale, too, is made palatable to the listeners in that Iphigenia does not die but is only whisked off to a far-away country.

The sacrificial motif is found also in circumcision. At least symbolically, something belonging to the newborn child must be sacrificed to God.

The Sacrifice

Like every major archetypal image, the image of sacrifice leads to caricature and excess. I am thinking of the thousands of human sacrificial victims which the Aztecs believed the Gods were requiring. To take an example closer to home: the millions of young men who died in battles of attrition during World War I can be understood as a horrendous caricature of the image of sacrifice. That generals and politicians were prepared to allow hundreds of thousands of young men to die for the sake of gaining a few square miles of terrain, and that hundreds of thousands of young men allowed themselves to be slaughtered, is hardly intelligible from a so-called rational point of view. This must have to do with a demonic possession through the archetypal image of sacrifice.

In this connection we must also recall the systematic murder of millions of European Jews by the German Nazis. Thousands, tens of thousands, millions allowed themselves to be driven by the torturers to sacrifice.

Every archetypal possibility becomes, when over-actualized, a horrendous demon.

When the thoughts and images of sacrifice are lived out as a caricature, people always react violently against them. In our day such a reaction is in full swing. The willingness to sacrifice, the joy of sacrifice, the readiness to sacrifice have all taken on, in certain circles, an obscene connotation. This does not change the fact that the sacrifice of something very dear to us appears to be indispensable for individuation, for the salvation of the soul.

I am thinking here of what has been for two thousand years the agreed-upon exemplar of the path to individuation in the Western world, namely, the life of Christ. In order to become one with the Father, Christ had to sacrifice everything: reputation, self-esteem and the esteem of others, life itself.

This book is attempting, among other things, to probe the individuational and salvational character of marriage. In the context of our present discussion, it goes without saying that great sacrifices are demanded also by marriage. Most married people must, to some extent, renounce certain parts of their personalities; they must sacrifice at the altar of marriage. Marriage is a continuous unevadable confrontation that can be resolved only through death. Such a long-term confrontation is possible, however, only if one or both of the marriage partners renounce something important. At first everything is confronted, but it soon becomes apparent to the marriage partners that this unevadable long-term confrontation can be maintained only if something essential of each person's own soul is consciously renounced.

A wife is musically gifted, for example, and out of love for her husband she renounces music because without her support he cannot advance professionally and would fall into depressions. Or, a husband must give up making anything of himself in the business world; he must place his light under a bushel so that his wife's light may shine more brightly.

Here is a dream that deals with this theme. The dreamer is a forty-year-old woman who has sacrificed her artistic abilities for her husband and her family. She did not develop her own artistic gifts but rather helped her husband who had a position of extraordinary responsibility. She supported him emotionally, listening to him for hours in the evenings as he told of his professional difficulties, disappointments, and successes. This is the dream: Her child, who bears a certain resemblance to Mr. W. (an artist with whom she is acquainted), is drowning or is at the point of drowning. The woman is in a state of panic, and she tries to save the child. Desperately she runs back and forth. The child, however, sinks deeper and deeper into the water. The woman runs onto some dam-like structures; on both sides of them is water, but in the middle are some ponds. The child is always in a different pool, and each time still deeper in water. The woman is not able to save the child. Finally she sees it in very deep water, and it is no longer moving.

Towards the end of the dream the woman had the impression of being an observer of the whole scene; she found herself somewhere above the whole happening, and she believed that she recognized the form of these dams.

As she thought about this dream afterwards, and about how the dam-like structures had looked from above, it suddenly occurred to her that the whole thing clearly represented a mandala. The dams were the drawn lines; the pools, the empty spaces in between.

The dream has the character of a nightmare. She could not prevent the child from drowning; on the other hand, the view from above filled her with deep peace.

We might ask ourselves if this dream is not an indication that the analysand has to sacrifice her own creativity in the Self, or for the Self. Usually such mandalas symbolize the meaningful structure and dynamics of the soul, the goal or the motivating power of individuation. This mandala contains the sacrifice.

Many marriages break up because the idea of sacrifice is rejected, and in this connection many analyses and psychotherapies have profoundly disturbing effects on marriage. In the name of the full development of the individual personality, of individual wholeness, the individuation marriage is sacrificed.

For reasons which are not fully apparent or accountable to me, this narcissistic development of personality and the enmity against any kind of sacrifice of personality are veritable dogmas of most modern psychotherapeutic groups; for this reason many marriages are disturbed in such groups. Perhaps such groups, if not properly led, are the unintentional, unconscious tools of the collective movements of the times; most probably, however, it is precisely in this strong constellation of the collective-unconscious dominants that the only therapeutic possibility of such groups lies: through them one can become conscious of the dominant collective images.

Again and again married people in middle age find their way to the psychologist, the marriage counselor, or the psychiatrist with the complaint: I cannot grow; I cannot develop my personality; I have to leave too many of my abilities lying fallow; I would like to break out and finally discover myself, finally be able to grow. The theme of the woman—or man—who breaks out of the narrow confines of marriage is a favorite in many novels, stories, and films.

Frequently, in the moment of truth, it comes down to nothing other than becoming aware of the necessity for sacrificing a portion of the individual's personality. One tries to evade this aspect of individuation. And there are today many psychologists to whom the individuation character of marriage is unknown, and who furthermore do not want to know anything about the necessity of sacrifice. They belong rather to the modern cult of personality, and are therefore in the service of well-being, rather than of salvation; in this area they can cause much mischief. Sacrifice is rejected out of hand; for dogmatic reasons it is not allowed to exist.

Obviously we are not speaking here of a moralistic, reproachful sacrifice in the spirit of martyrdom. This concerns rather the freely-willed sacrifice, without reproach to anyone; it concerns the renunciation necessary to and helpful for individuation.

In this regard, even sexuality must be sacrificed in certain marriages. I am touching here on the problems of frigidity and impotence. Persons who have been struck by Eros' leaden arrow can often be healed by psychotherapy or by lessons in sexual techniques; often, however, nothing helps. It is unfortunate that the sexually-able partner is then often advised to seek love somewhere else. The solution to the problem is certainly not this simple. Either the one must renounce sexuality, or the other must give up the fidelity of his partner. The sacrifice of sexuality is just as meaningful as its enactment. Or the indifferent partner must sacrifice to his individuation companion his aversion to sexuality. In this way, the greatest of all sexual anomalies, frigidity and impotence in marriage, can be accepted under the aspect of salvation.

I have described sexuality as instinctive individuation, and the confrontation-marriage as chosen individuation. Both forms of individuation are closely related and are often experienced together. These two forms of individuation can strengthen and enrich one another. But their intimate coupling also leads to many tragedies and to many misunderstandings. The one path to individuation does not guarantee the other. And the one must not be confused with the other. Psychologically we must clearly distinguish the two ways in life and in awareness.

Many young people decide to get married out of sexual

passion. An erotic intoxication is something so gripping that it seriously impairs the ability to make such distinctions. Nevertheless many young people have the sure instinct to recognize whether their "being-in-love" is primarily a sexual intoxication, or whether their "love" also includes the enthusiasm of moving together with a partner onto the path of individuation-via-marriage.

It is often believed, however, that the one individuation pathway can lay claim to the other. Many married partners believe, for example, that they have the right to demand sexual fulfillment by virtue of the individuation pathway of marriage. The reverse is also frequently the case: partners who find themselves only on the instinctual, sexual pathway to individuation unjustifiably require the conscious, chosen individuation pathway of marriage.

DIVORCE

Before going further I would like to take up the subject of divorce, the possible dissolution of marriage.

Marriage lasts until death. One enters into it with this intention. Its deeper significance is the unevadable, life-long confrontation. The individuation pathway of marriage consists in the fact that in it one cannot evade the dialectical encounter with the partner, even when things become difficult and unpleasant.

This by no means implies, however, that divorce should not exist, or that divorce violates certain claims and demands of individuation. First of all, as I have already indicated, it does imply that it would be better perhaps if fewer people got married. The unmarried state should once more be given a higher value. It is to be hoped that our contemporary world will once again increase the socially sanctioned possibilities of being single *and* respected. It is to be further hoped that being single would then not necessitate living asexually. New forms of living together do after all seem to be coming into existence—communes, for example, or other communities which do not possess the exclusive character of marriage. It would also be desirable for more women to be able to become happy mothers without having to get married. It is injurious to the individuation pathway of marriage that many people, particularly women, submit themselves to this institution of salvation in order to have children and to be mothers. For people whose main interest is the next generation, marriage is a totally unsuitable institution.

Errare humanum est. It can become clear to married people sooner or later that they are not suited to their individuation partner, even if serious misunderstandings do not exist between them. Perhaps one has not found the right partner for the salvation pathway of marriage, or one discovers that one is completely unsuited for this particular pathway. The criterion for whether or not to divorce should not be sought in the degree of difficulty or pathology in the marriage, but rather should clearly depend on whether or not the marriage represents for both partners a pathway of salvation.

Before the partners notice the problem, however, they have become parents. The question then arises: should we stay together for the sake of the children?

My opinion is that no consideration whatsoever should be given to the children. I hold this opinion for the following reasons.

First of all, it is extraordinarily difficult to know exactly what hurts children psychologically and what helps them. Does it damage the children to grow up in an intact family in which the parents are playing a farce to them? Does it help them if they see how the parents are sacrificing themselves for the welfare of the children while renouncing their own pathways to individuation? Or do they develop better in an honest situation, which a divorce often clarifies for them? We can present here only the supposition—which observation has often confirmed—that it is a heavy burden for children to witness how the parents reject their own salvation and their own individuation. This creates in the children a chronically bad conscience toward their parents and awakens out of this bad conscience an unhealthy aggression.

Moreover, the opinion that one must unconditionally stay married because of children, even when it is acknowledged that the marriage is not an individuation pathway, is too much bound to "well-being." Marriage is not an institution for well-being, and this goes for the children as well as for the parents. The important thing is to exemplify for the children the possibilities of individuation. We should demonstrate to our children the importance of salvation, not of well-being. It is therefore highly questionable whether it is right for us to devote ourselves, by hypocritically staying together, to the service of well-being rather than to the knowledge of salvation. We want to direct our children to salvation and not to well-being. The distinction between salvation and well-being is of the greatest importance precisely here, in connection with what is supposed to happen to our children and how we must conduct ourselves toward them.

Just another small warning regarding the circumstances of

those who find individuation in their marriage and those for whom it lies elsewhere. People seek their salvation on various paths. It is terribly difficult, however, for anyone not to proselytize, consciously or unconsciously, for his own way. This often leads to unfortunate developments, above all when a person exercises great influence on another, whether it be as analyst, psychological counselor, or influential friend. We are never objective, even when we believe we are, not even as psychologists. There is the sacred way of marriage and there is the sacred way of being single. "Disciples" of each way try to convert one another—and often cause damage thereby. A divorced woman who, after bitter experience, finds out that marriage is not her way will eagerly offer herself as friendly advisor to married people who are having problems, and she will tend towards converting those who seek out her advice to her own kind of non-marital individuation. And suddenly the couple who has been looking for help gets a divorce. Therapists and marriage counselors also act as missionaries, whether they want to or not. It would be good if therapists were conscious of their achieved or lost individuation pathways, and if they could admit any biases to those who come seeking their help; this would make it possible for those who are looking for advice to protect themselves against the conscious or unconscious missionary tendencies of the counselor.

I would like to imagine that an analyst for whom marriage represents a failed pathway to individuation would say to his patient when he begins to speak of marriage difficulties: "Marriage is not my way, so be careful that I do not convert you to a marriageless life."

SALVATION, WELL-BEING, INDIVIDUATION: ONLY FOR THE EDUCATED?

I have spoken in this book explicitly about well-being, salvation, individuation, and other such topics. One could ask himself whether it is even possible for the average man to understand such complicated concepts or to direct himself by them. One would ask if there really are many married couples who reflect on whether or not they have found in marriage their pathway of salvation, their pathway of individuation; or whether it is not the case that many more understand marriage as a welfare agency.

As a psychologist I am not trying to force anything on anyone or to bring him to the point where he can toss around absolute concepts. On the contrary, the psychologist seeks to understand what is happening, what drives people and motivates them, and to find names for the psychological phenomena. The psychological phenomenon is experienced imagistically by most people, not described intellectually. Until recently it was above all the religions and the churches which supplied people with images through which they were empowered to reflect upon their fundamental spiritual concerns.

It is the case that salvation and well-being are fundamental psychological motivations for every person, even if the person does not become conscious of them in a conceptual way. Thus marriage partners, be they psychologically educated or uneducated, be they literate or illiterate, ask themselves if marriage serves well-being more, or salvation more; if one should stay together for the sake of the children's welfare, or if one should seek salvation.

118

Only For The Educated?

That this is in fact the case we see again and again in the dreams and fantasies of people whom we meet, no matter what their social heritage, no matter what their education.

To give an example: A twenty-two-year-old industrial seamstress told me the following story: "My father left us when I was ten years old. He sent my mother money regularly; however, he only visited us children every one or two years. I loved my mother very much. I criticized my father severely when he left us. We had to live very poorly, and none of us children could stay in school after the age of twelve. But in spite of all the criticisms I also love my father very much. I don't know why. After all, he left me. When I would see him from time to time—it was seldom enough— he didn't take much interest in me. He always told about his job; only that interested him. He is crazy. My grandmother also says that he is a little crazy. But she also likes him. I wouldn't want to have any other father.'

It seems to me that from this woman's story we may at least approach the psychological facts. The father's fulfillment, the father's salvation and the father's individuation lie elsewhere than in marriage. It seems to be tied up with his occupational life. The daughter accepts this and grasps it and does not reject her father; she even admires him in a way. She has the impression that he was true to something, even though she does not understand it fully.

MARRIAGE IS DEAD, LONG LIVE MARRIAGE!

At the beginning of this book I referred to the image of the turbulent divine marriage of Zeus and Hera. These two did not enjoy a so-called happy marriage; they not only loved each other, they also fought each other in the most vicious ways. This couple can help us to understand marriage from a new standpoint.

There is no shortage of efforts to illuminate and grasp the contemporary marriage. There is also no shortage of efforts to help individual married couples to overcome their problems. What is lacking, in my opinion, is research which would reveal under which star, under which images, our theoretical and practical work on marriage is actually taking place. If we want to understand other people and our own work psychologically, it is essential first of all to become clear as to which Gods we are serving, to which images we are duty-bound. It can even turn out that we are serving two masters, that we are being led by contradictory images, and thus causing great confusion.

Many of the pains and efforts taken to deal with the contemporary marriage are dominated by considerations of well-being, happiness, and biology. This corresponds to the position of contemporary psychology, which distinguishes itself through a very deep skepticism, amounting even to a rejection, of anything transcendent.

Many professionals who concern themselves with marriage, be they psychologists or marriage counselors, have as their goal the so-called normal, happy marriage, the non-neurotic relationship between two more or less healthy marriage partners. To reach this goal, much is undertaken. Techniques are worked out which supposedly help married people understand one another better, physically and psychologically. An attempt is made to explain the neurotic mechanisms of relating to the partner, to expose such mechanisms, to change them or eliminate them. Marriage is understood as a relationship between two people which, through psychological efforts on the part of the married persons, and perhaps with the help of professionals, can be shaped into something satisfying and happy.

All of these efforts, however, do not alter the fact that divorces continue to occur and that existing marriages often appear to be terribly sick. Out of honest despair, then, the radical alteration or even dissolution of this institution is often demanded. Most people expect to be able to lead a happy married life, but few couples are capable of doing so. Thus the legitimate question arises as to whether it would not be better to proceed radically and put an end to marriage. The case for this viewpoint becomes stronger now that many of the factors which supported marriage at least outwardly are slowly falling by the wayside. Very few married people run a farm or a business together anymore, and consequently few understand their marriage and shape their marriage as a business partnership. More than ninety percent of the working population are employees. The care of children unites married people for some twenty years, while most of them have to live together for fifty or sixty years.

To this we must add that many psychologists are of the opinion that parents are fundamentally not suited to raise their children, especially if they are, like most people, living in an arduous and problematic marriage. Then too, it is possible for only very few persons today to engage in power politics through marriage. Ever fewer economic, social, and political factors seem to be coming to the aid of marriage.

For this reason the last remaining support, sexuality, is all the more convulsively fastened onto. In this area one finds countless books which want to teach married people how to lead a happy, full, sexual life. Aphrodite is supposed to supply the plaster and mortar for the collapsing house of marriage, and to help hold it together. Marriage is in fact a place where sexuality can often be intensely lived out. In recent times, however, marriage has lost its monopoly in this regard. Young people have become sexually freer. More and more they can live out their sexuality without becoming maritally bound to one another. All assiduous attempts to limit extramarital life, or to eliminate it through the prohibition of concubinage or similar arrangements, end up failing miserably. More and more it is possible for members of all social classes to lead a satisfying sexual life without getting married. What only twenty years ago seemed impossible is today firmly established: even so-called decent young men and women from stable families can live together so long as it suits them without further ado.

Further still, it is becoming increasingly well-known that marriage can have an inhibitive effect on sexuality. For many people marriage signifies, not the place for living out sexuality, but rather the place of sexual frustration. Thus it seems that even the last support of marriage, outside of having children, is slowly losing its efficacy. Marriage as conceived under the image of well-being has become, for countless people, the greatest disappointment.

The so-called happy marriage is unequivocally finished. Marriage as a welfare institution has no justification anymore. Psychologists who feel themselves committed to the goal of well-being would do better, if they really took their standpoint seriously, to recommend and suggest other forms of living together, rather than to waste their energy trying to patch up a fundamentally impossible institution with a lot of technical treatment modalities. From the viewpoint of well-being, marriage is not only a patient, it is a mortally-ill patient—which should not be begrudged its death as soon as possible.

Here and there attempts are made to define marriage in a new way, using the interpersonal relationship as a starting point. The interpersonal relationship is today something like a God. And there are theologians who argue that God shows himself in, or consists of, the interpersonal relationship. But so-called interpersonal relationships can be built up and tended to outside of marriage. For a happy interpersonal relationship, marriage is more likely to be a poor setting. One lives too closely together and rubs against the other too vigorously.

In my practice I have made the following remarkable observation: the level of difficulty in a marriage, the sum of suffering, irritation, anger, and frustration, also the neurotic and perverse elements which are to be found in a marriage—all these do not necessarily parallel a tendency towards dissolution of the marriage. That is to say, outwardly-bad marriages are often clearly viable and actually continue until the death of one of the partners. On the other hand, less problematic marriages, those which contain less pathology, often show a tendency towards dissolution; they seem to dissolve more readily than do the more difficult marriages. The observer who sails under the flag of well-being has difficulty understanding this. His tendency is to give those marriages in which neuroses, sexual perversions, twisted relationships, and similar phenomena appear, a bad prognosis.

The tenacity of marriage as an institution, the fact that it continues to be popular despite its pain-inflicting structure, becomes easier to understand if we turn our attention to images that have nothing to do with well-being.

The central issue in marriage is not well-being or happiness; it is, as this book has tried to demonstrate, salvation. Marriage involves not only a man and a woman who happily love each other and raise offspring together, but rather two people who are trying to individuate, to find their "soul's salvation." Perhaps this sounds pious and old-fashioned. Out of genuine anxiety that religious elements might becloud or falsify our scientific understanding, we have closed off the approach to an understanding of the soul; thus we hold before our eyes an image of man that is only one among many. We are creatures who are oriented not only towards well-being; we are creatures whose behavior cannot be simply explained as a striving for survival and happiness, for release of tension and contentment. We are not merely Phaeaces. The result of this is that man and—what interests us particularly here—one of his most important institutions, marriage, impresses us for the most part as sick. Marriage is judged by the images of well-being and comes off poorly.

Marriage as such is defined not only by images of well-being but also by those of salvation. The conception "till death do us part" has nothing to do with well-being; seen from the viewpoint of well-being, the notion "till death" makes no sense. Considered from the viewpoint of well-being, marriage is incurably sick. For this reason, efforts to expose and to remove the so-called neuroticisms of marriage partners and of marriage itself have only a limited value; much that is seen as sick by the apostles of well-being is not sick at all, e.g., the above-mentioned "sacrifice of an important, creative portion of the personality."

For people who worship at the altar of well-being, marriage makes for illness. And this is true not only for these people. The roads to salvation are many; there are as many individuation pathways as there are people. Marriage is one salvation pathway among many, although it contains many different possibilities.

For this reason I alluded at the beginning of this book to many different images of marriage. Zeus and Hera offer one image, the holy family another; there are still others, and every married couple has its own balance, its variation of the marriage image. The married couple that is stamped by the image of the holy family experiences the devotees of Zeus and Hera as abnormal; to Hera and Zeus, the holy family would seem to be a pitiful business. Salvation pathways have always been very particular. I am thinking of the "holy ones" who sit for years atop a pole in order to find their salvation, or of the medieval nuns who would kiss the wounds of lepers. So too we find a great wealth of different "individuation pathways of marriage:" for instance, the prince-consort marriage wherein the wife rules and the husband serves quietly behind the scenes, or the Mafia marriage in which the husband is a gangster in the outer world but lives out the holy-family marriage with his wife and children, and many more.

To understand people and their social structures requires a vision of the images which are at work in the background. The phenomenon of marriage cannot be grasped without considering the images which give marriage its form. Every psychological manifestation must be confronted with its own images and not with images that are foreign to it. Gothic cathedrals, if confronted with idealized images from the world of ancient Greece, seem unintelligible or debased. In the foregoing pages I have tried to show how holding on to an inadequate image—reproduction—obscures the true proportions of sexuality. Sexuality, however, is powerful and instinctual; this individuation pathway and its symbolism are able to maintain themselves whether they are recognized or not.

As people who are members of cultural, religious, and national communities, and as marriage partners, we have created and continue to create the possibilities of individuation, of the quest for salvation, through marriage. The images which stand behind marriage as we understand it today are various different images of individuation, of salvation. As soon as we confront concrete marriages with other, foreign images—such as well-being, happiness, a home for children—marriage appears to be senseless, withered, moribund, and kept alive largely by a great apparatus of psychologists and marriage counselors.

Marriage is dead; marriage lives.

Books of Permanent Jungian Interest

God and the Unconscious
Victor White

In chapters titled "Psychotherapy and Ethics," "Devils and Complexes," "Revelation and the Unconscious," and "Gnosis, Gnosticism and Faith," Victor White, friend, colleague—and at times sharp critic—of Jung's, explores the relationship between theology and psychology. Includes a foreword by Jung and a new introduction by the poet William Everson, in whose life Victor White played a pivotal role. A classic of Jungian psychology. Indexes. (xxxiii, 245 pp./ISBN 0-88214-503-7)

Incest and Human Love
Robert Stein

Presents a new and radical model for psychotherapy that values erotic differentiation more than the expansion of ego control. Stein's vision emerges out of a sustained examination of the Incest Taboo, which he regards as the key to psychological development, showing its relevance to work, fantasy, and culture as well as to relationships in marriage, in the family, and between patient and analyst. Uncompromising in its challenge to conventional ego psychology, Jungian conservatism, Freudian reductionism, and to every school of thought that veers away from the animal level of the human soul. (200 pp./ISBN 0-88214-506-1)

Insearch: Psychology and Religion
James Hillman

Widely used in pastoral counseling and psychotherapeutic training, this book sets out the fundamental principles and attitudes of Jungian psychology in a simple, yet deeply experiential style. "Probably Hillman's most humanly feeling book . . . recommended for dream interpretation and practical examples." Although translated into Dutch, German, Japanese, and Italian, the original edition had been out of print for years. (126 pp./ ISBN 0-88214-501-0)

Animus and Anima
Emma Jung

Two classic papers on the elemental persons of the psyche. Examines both animus and anima as they appear in behavior, fantasies, dreams, and mythology. Accessible, incisive, and with plenty of practical counsel, this book maps a way toward the union of opposites and the emergence of the Self. Includes a picture of the author. (94 pp./ ISBN 0-88214-301-8)

An Introduction to the Interpretation of Fairytales
Marie-Louise von Franz

The basic course for a psychological understanding of fairytales. Includes a review of the literature, various theories of fairytales, an examination in detail of one example, and a long chapter on the shadow, animus and anima. Index. (160 pp./ISBN 0-88214-101-5)

Spring Publications, Inc. • *P.O. Box 222069* • *Dallas, Texas 75222*